Jane Goodall

AVAILABLE UP CLOSE TITLES:

RACHEL CARSON by Ellen Levine

JOHNNY CASH by Anne E. Neimark

ELLA FITZGERALD by Tanya Lee Stone

JANE GOODALL by Sudipta Bardhan-Quallen

ROBERT F. KENNEDY by Marc Aronson

THURGOOD MARSHALL by Chris Crowe

ELVIS PRESLEY by Wilborn Hampton

JOHN STEINBECK by Milton Meltzer

OPRAH WINFREY by Ilene Cooper

FRANK LLOYD WRIGHT by Jan Adkins

FUTURE UP CLOSE TITLES:

W. E. B. DU BOIS by Tonya Bolden

BILL GATES by Marc Aronson

HARPER LEE by Kerry Madden

RONALD REAGAN by James Sutherland

BABE RUTH by Wilborn Hampton

UP*close:*

Jane Goodall

a twentieth-century life by
SUDIPTA BARDHAN-QUALLEN

VIKING

VIKING

Published by Penguin Group

Penguin Young Readers Group, 345 Hudson Street, New York, New York 10014, U.S.A.

Penguin Group (Canada), 90 Eglinton Avenue East, Suite 700, Toronto, Ontario,
Canada M4P 2Y3 (a division of Pearson Penguin Canada Inc.)

Penguin Books Ltd, 80 Strand, London WC2R 0RL, England

Penguin Ireland, 25 St Stephen's Green, Dublin 2, Ireland (a division of Penguin Books Ltd)

Penguin Group (Australia), 250 Camberwell Road, Camberwell, Victoria 3124, Australia
(a division of Pearson Australia Group Pty Ltd)

Penguin Books India Pvt Ltd, 11 Community Centre, Panchsheel Park, New Delhi – 110 017, India

Penguin Group (NZ), 67 Apollo Drive, Rosedale, North Shore 0632, New Zealand
(a division of Pearson New Zealand Ltd)

Penguin Books (South Africa) (Pty) Ltd, 24 Sturdee Avenue, Rosebank, Johannesburg 2196,
South Africa

Penguin Books Ltd, Registered Offices: 80 Strand, London WC2R 0RL, England

First published in 2008 by Viking, a division of Penguin Young Readers Group

10 9 8 7 6 5 4 3 2 1

LIBRARY OF CONGRESS CATALOGING-IN-PUBLICATION DATA
Bardhan-Quallen, Sudipta.
Up close Jane Goodall / by Sudipta Bardhan. – 1st ed.
p. cm.
ISBN 978-0-670-06263-8 (hardcover)
1. Goodall, Jane, 1934–Biography–Juvenile literature. 2. Primatologists–England–Biography–
Juvenile literature. 3. Women primatologists–England–Biography–Juvenile literature.
4. Chimpanzees–Tanzania–Gombe Stream National Park–Juvenile literature. I. Title.
QL31.G58B37 2008
590.92–dc22
[B]
2007038206

Printed in the U.S.A.
Set in Goudy
Book design by Jim Hoover

Contents

Jane Goodall

Foreword

I MET JANE GOODALL in 1984. I was six and a half years old, and she was on TV. My parents were picky about what I could watch, but a National Geographic special was acceptable. The show was called *Among the Wild Chimpanzees*—and I was hooked. The first time she materialized out of the jumble of leaves and branches, I thought that she must have been the bravest woman in the world. When I saw her sitting within just a few feet of wild chimps, I *knew* she must have been the bravest woman in the world.

On TV, the chimps were fascinating, with complex lives and emotions. My cousin, who in my mind knew everything—he was in *college!*—laughingly told me that chimps were just mindless brutes. I didn't understand how anyone could have thought that. Jane walked among them with ease, as if she was following children instead of wild animals. By the end of the documentary, Jane was my new hero. I admired her tenacity, her determination, and her intelligence. I began to read everything I could about Jane and her work, even checking out a worn, dog-eared copy of her book *In the Shadow of Man* from the library. I vowed that someday I would follow in Jane's footsteps.

Though I didn't grow up to be Jane Goodall, I did travel to Africa—not to Gombe, but to Botswana and South Africa. It was very different from Jane's experience—I honestly don't have the bravery to sleep on a camp cot in a tent, with nothing between me and wild animals but a stretch of canvas. And I can't imagine living for months with no electricity, no running water, and no wireless Internet!

I did, however, get to experience the adventure of seeing Africa in all its wild glory. One night I was able to watch a herd of elephants, mothers and babies, converge on a watering hole at sunset. When our Land Rover ventured a bit too close, one of the humongous mothers turned and glared, a warning to us to stay back. The rest of the herd continued, unbothered, to drink and splash in the waning light. It was one of the most spectacular sights I had ever seen in my life. I thought back for a moment to the little girl who had been so captivated by Jane Goodall's pioneering and courageous work at Gombe, and I felt as if I had, in a very small way, shared in the thrill Jane must have experienced.

Introduction

ALL DAY, JANE GOODALL had scoured the terrain of the Gombe Stream Chimpanzee Reserve. She scrambled up and down the rugged trails, over the mountain slopes, and through the forested valleys. Since dawn that morning she had been on her feet, yet she still had not spotted a single chimpanzee.

Soon she reached the Peak, a high spot with a marvelous view of the land below. The Peak was Jane's favorite spot to go looking for chimpanzees. Since it was almost five o'clock in the evening, Jane knew there was not much more daylight left. She would have to stop her observations and head back to camp soon. Hopefully, she could catch a glimpse

The chimpanzee Jane called David Greybeard reaches for her hand. David was one of the first chimps to trust Jane.

of a chimp making a night nest in a tree before the darkness forced her to go home.

A scream pierced the air—Jane recognized it as the cry of a young chimpanzee. She scanned the horizon with her binoculars and soon spotted a group of four chimps quarreling over some fruit. The argument quickly ended, and the group settled in to eat peacefully.

Jane carefully made her way closer to the chimps. For ten minutes she crept silently toward a gnarled old fig tree—but by the time she arrived, the chimps were gone. Depression began to overcome Jane; despite her best efforts, the apes had realized she was approaching and departed.

Then something caught Jane's eye. Less than twenty yards away, two male chimps were staring directly at her. She recognized the one she had named David Greybeard and the other as his constant companion Goliath. Jane braced herself for the chimps' inevitable flight and escape, since every chimp she approached always had.

This time, however, was different. David and Goliath merely stared, even when Jane slowly sat down. After a few moments, the two apes began to groom each other. Two more chimpanzees soon materialized—a female and a young ape. Jane turned in their direction; they dipped down out of sight, only to reappear forty yards away. They, too, watched Jane silently.

Jane wrote that "for over half a year I had been trying to overcome the chimpanzees' inherent fear of me, the fear which made them vanish into the undergrowth whenever I approached. . . . Now two males were sitting so close that I could almost hear them breathing." For ten minutes David and Goliath continued to groom. Then David stood and stared directly at Jane. Her shadow fell over him; Jane sat terrified that the small change in the light would be enough to spook him. It did not, and when Jane hurried back to camp that night, she reveled in the triumph of the day.

"ADVENTURES OF TARZAN"

The Wild Animal Serial Supreme

STARRING

Elmo Lincoln

IN

15 Electrifying Episodes

PRODUCED BY
GREAT WESTERN PRODUCING CO.
For WEISS BROTHERS'
NUMA PICTURES CORP.

PICTURIZED FROM THE CONCLUDING CHAPTERS OF
"THE RETURN OF TARZAN"
By

Edgar Rice Burroughs

LIONS, ELEPHANTS, CROCODILES, LEOPARDS, APES, MONKEYS AND A HOST OF OTHER JUNGLE DENIZENS. SCENE AFTER SCENE OF THRILLING EXCITEMENT IN EACH EPISODE OF "ADVENTURES OF TARZAN." THE HEROIC LINCOLN AS TARZAN THE APE-MAN, IS THE CENTRAL FIGURE IN A SERIES OF HAIR-BREADTH ESCAPES AND WONDERFUL STUNTS WHICH WILL KEEP YOU ON THE EDGE OF YOUR CHAIR THROUGHOUT THE ENTIRE SERIAL.

"THE TARZAN OF TARZANS"

One

MARGARET MYFANWE JOSEPH often heard admirers compare her to a green-eyed goddess. Vanne, as she was called by everyone, had fine features, rich chestnut hair, and a warm smile. When her future husband, Mortimer Herbert Morris-Goodall, saw her walking one evening near his London apartment, he fell off the stairs—just to get her attention.

Mortimer was blue-eyed, blond, tall, and handsome. He and Vanne quickly became friends, and eventually they married. Though they got along well, the two were sort of a mismatched pair. Vanne was quiet and somewhat solitary, and dreamed of being a writer someday. Mortimer, on the other hand, had a passion for machines and technology, especially fast

Edgar Rice Burroughs's books about Tarzan made a lasting impression on Jane, who was an avid reader.

cars. He drove an Aston Martin racer and lived what Vanne described as a "whirly kind of life."

Vanne did not share her husband's love for race cars, though she supported Mortimer as he tried to build a career as a race car driver. In 1933 he was asked to join the team of Aston Martins in the Le Mans Grand Prix d'Endurance, one of the sport's most grueling races. Drivers were expected to race as many laps as they could in twenty-four hours, from four o'clock one afternoon to the same time the next day. Mortimer did well enough in that race to join the Aston Martin team, kicking off his professional race car–driving career. The couple must have celebrated Mortimer's good fortune—approximately nine months later, on April 3, 1934, at around 11:30 at night, the Morris-Goodalls welcomed their first child into the world. The baby, a girl, was named Valerie Jane.

It was clear from an early age that Valerie Jane had a particular affinity for animals. For her first birthday, Mortimer bought his daughter a special toy—a lifelike, child-sized, stuffed chimpanzee named Jubilee, in honor of a baby chimp that had been born at the

London Zoo. The toy had shining button eyes; soft, dark brown fur; and a white, downy chin. It played music when its tummy was squeezed. Several friends warned Mortimer and Vanne that Valerie Jane would surely be frightened by a toy so lifelike. But Valerie Jane loved Jubilee so much that she toted it everywhere and put it in cast-off dresses. Later, her family would remember Valerie Jane's love for Jubilee as a sign of things to come.

After Valerie Jane was born, the Morris-Goodalls' family life became more tense. Mortimer proved to be a better race car driver than he was a husband and father. He was careless with money, and bills often went unpaid. Mortimer worked much of the day at his engineering job and often saw his daughter only when she was sleeping. This added to the growing distance between him and his daughter. In fact, his contribution to Valerie Jane's life came mostly in the things she had inherited from him at birth—good health, high energy, a sense of competitiveness, and a willingness to take risks. Almost everything else about Valerie Jane could be credited to Vanne.

Vanne, together with the family's nanny, Nancy

Sowden, was responsible for Valerie Jane's everyday life. Vanne believed in raising children with love and reasoned discipline, and she taught Valerie Jane to appreciate the natural world and the quiet pleasures that it could provide.

As Valerie Jane grew, Jubilee continued to be a regular companion, but the little girl's interest in animals had plenty of opportunities to flourish. The garden of the house was a new frontier full of friends; and Valerie Jane enjoyed the company of flowers, birds, insects, a pet tortoise named Johnny Walker, a dog named Peggy, and the many other animals she discovered.

When she was eighteen months old, Valerie Jane dug up a handful of earthworms. She took them home and carried them into her bed, despite Nanny Sowden's disgust. When her mother checked on Valerie Jane, the toddler was lying happily side by side with the worms. At that point, Vanne gently told Valerie Jane that the worms would die away from the earth. The little girl sighed and hurried back to the garden to return the animals to their home.

A short time after the earthworm incident, the Morris-Goodalls visited the seaside at Cornwall. Valerie Jane spent the day collecting seashells—which turned out to be yellow sea snails that began crawling all around the house. Vanne once again explained to Valerie Jane that the snails would die unless they were returned to the sea. The girl became hysterical with worry, and everyone in the house had to help collect the snails and return them to safety before Valerie Jane would calm down.

Valerie Jane basked in love and attention from Vanne and Nanny, and grew a bit spoiled. So when Judith Daphne Morris-Goodall was born precisely on Valerie Jane's fourth birthday, April 3, 1938, she reacted with jealousy. As an adult, she remembered, "I went berserk for a while. I became very unmanageable and wild. I did awful things." One day when Nanny took Valerie Jane and the baby, called Judy, for a walk, the older sister kept screaming the most disgusting word she could think of: *diarrhea*! Eventually, Valerie Jane and Judy became dear playmates, but it took some time for the older girl to get used to sharing the spotlight in the Morris-Goodall household.

When Valerie Jane was five years old and Judy was a little more than one, Mortimer decided to focus on racing full-time, so the Morris-Goodall family sold their house and moved to France. At first they were happy in their villa near the seaside resort of Le Touquet. The girls enjoyed the sunshine-filled life in the country, and the family had many visitors to the villa to keep them busy. Within a few months of their settling in France, however, it became impossible for the Morris-Goodalls to stay there. It was the summer of 1939, and German forces under Adolf Hitler had begun the initial invasions that would result in World War II. France was no longer safe for the Morris-Goodalls. Vanne immediately sent Nanny Sowden and her daughters back to England to live with Mortimer's mother, Elizabeth Nutt, in the countryside.

Valerie Jane could not pronounce the word *granny*, so she and everyone in the family called Elizabeth "Danny Nutt." During their stay there, Danny Nutt gave her older granddaughter the responsibility of collecting the hens' eggs. Since she loved animals, Valerie Jane was eager to do her job well, but she soon became perplexed by the process of egg laying. She did not understand where there could be an opening in a hen's body large enough for an egg to pass through, so she decided to investigate on her own.

Valerie Jane's first attempt ended in failure when she was shooed away by the hen's terrified squawking. Next, she decided that if she was in the henhouse before the hen walked in, she would not cause a stir. She waited silently inside a second, empty henhouse, hoping that another hen would arrive to lay her eggs.

While Valerie Jane investigated the mystery of the hens, her family discovered that the little girl was missing. The police were called, and family members and neighbors frantically searched for her. Oblivious to the hullabaloo, Valerie Jane remained in the henhouse until, at last, a hen came inside and settled down on a nest. Later, she remembered, "I must have kept very still or she would have been disturbed. Presently the hen half stood and I saw a round white object gradually protruding from the feathers between her legs. Suddenly, with a plop, the egg landed on the straw." She had solved the mystery.

After her discovery, Valerie Jane ran home. It had been almost four hours and had grown dark by then. The girl's hair and clothes were littered with straw from the henhouse, but what Vanne noticed most was her daughter's excitement. Rather than scolding her for causing such a fuss, Vanne listened carefully as Valerie Jane described what she had learned from watching the hen. In later years, Jane recalled, "If you look back on it with hindsight, that is the exact makings of a little scientist, curiosity, asking questions, watching. If you don't get the answer to the question, find out a way of doing it, so you are finding out for yourself. If that doesn't work, try again." Her mother's encouragement toward making new discoveries would be an important part of Jane's future work with animals.

Soon after the henhouse experiment, Mortimer joined the British army. He signed up with the Royal Engineers' Stevedore Battalion, and he left England in December 1939 to serve his country in the war effort. Vanne and her daughters did not remain at the Manor House. Her mother, Elizabeth Hornby Legarde Joseph, lived in a Victorian house in Bournemouth, England, called the Birches. Vanne moved herself and the girls into the Birches, which became home for Valerie Jane for the rest of her childhood.

Valerie Jane gave Vanne's mother the nickname Danny as well, and everyone called her that. Danny also opened her home to Vanne's sisters, Olwen (Olly) and Audrey (Audey). Vanne's brother, Eric, was a surgeon who visited the Birches on most weekends, but for the most part, the home was an all-female place, with Danny at the helm. An advantage to growing up in such an environment was that no one ever told Valerie Jane that she could not do something just because she was a girl.

At the age of eight, Valerie Jane discovered *The Story of Dr. Dolittle*, about a man who could speak with animals. To an animal lover such as Valerie Jane, Dr. Dolittle was living a dream life. Soon afterward, she found Edgar Rice Burroughs's books about Tarzan of the Apes. She remembered that "it was my imagination that created the Tarzan with whom I fell passionately in love, age ten. . . . So I felt that I would have been a much better mate for Tarzan than that wimpy Jane of his; I was terribly jealous of Jane, and that was when I got this dream: when I grew up, I would go to Africa, live with animals and write books about them."

Valerie Jane filled much of her time with fantasies of Africa and Tarzan, but there were harsh realities to face as well. Mortimer was almost completely absent, because he continued to serve abroad in the army. Eric and Olly both performed air-raid duties, which meant that when the air-raid sirens sounded, they had to leave home to help others. American soldiers frequently occupied the road outside the Birches. The girls sometimes befriended them before they were sent off to the front.

In 1945, Valerie Jane began to attend the Uplands Girls School in Parkstone, near Bournemouth. All the girls there wore uniforms consisting of a navy blue skirt with navy blue knickers underneath, a blouse with a white collar, and a belted tunic over the blouse. She privately called the school Countess Hoffan'on, and she described it in a letter to her friend Sally Cary: "We have lovely gym there, bars, horses, ropes and every thing else. Some of the girls are quite nice, others very nice, and others simply stinking (excuse my word please)." Between schoolwork and riding lessons on Saturdays, Valerie Jane's days were busy.

On school holidays, when Sally and her sister Susie came to visit at the Birches, Valerie Jane indulged her continuing love for animals. She organized a nature club called the Alligator Society. Valerie Jane had

strict rules for joining—each girl had to be able to rec-
ognize ten birds, ten dogs, ten trees, and five butter-
flies or moths. In a 1946 letter, she sent instructions to
Sally about making identification badges for the group:
"Find a fairly small alligator and trace it out and pin it
onto some green material. Cut round the edge of the
paper, so that you have a green cloth Alligator. Cover
the cardboard with white cloth and stitch the alligator
onto it. Put a safety pin in the back. As all the badges
must be the same send me a tracing of the Alligator
you use and also a piece of the paper the sieze [sic]
of the card board. . . . As I am the leader I will give
my Alligator an eye and you must not." As the oldest,
Valerie Jane was the natural leader, and she expected
to be obeyed. Judy remembered, "She was bossy, yes,
but she did have good ideas and she did organize fun
things. Occasionally, I'd say, 'No,' and then she was
very puzzled."

As the leader of the Alligator Society, Valerie
Jane also gave herself the code name Red Admiral
(the name of an eye-catching butterfly). Sally's code
name was Puffin, Susie's was Ladybird, and Judy's was
Trout. All four girls worked together on the *Alligator*

Society Magazine—a collection of nature articles that they wrote and compiled—and they had an Alligator camp in the garden of the Birches. When the girls were apart during school terms, the club continued through letters and occasional nature quizzes by mail.

In 1951, when Valerie Jane was seventeen years old, Vanne and Mortimer divorced. It wasn't much of a change for Valerie Jane, since Mortimer had been gone so much during the war. Larger changes in her life came with the end of her school days, when she began to refer to herself only as Jane. Somewhere along the line, she had decided that she did not like the name Valerie and dropped it. She felt much more comfortable being Jane.

With graduation upon her, Jane began to think about her future and what she would do with her life. Her examination scores were high enough to qualify her for the university, but her family could not afford the tuition. Jane enjoyed reading and writing, so she considered a career in journalism. She still dreamed of traveling to Africa to study animals, though, and in the end, Africa was too much of a draw for Jane to think about anything that might not help her get there.

At the time, women generally became teachers, nurses, or secretaries. Even if Jane could have found a way to study biology, field biology the way she imagined it simply did not exist. People—and always these people were men—who wanted to study animals did so in zoos with captive specimens. No one actually traveled to Africa to observe animals in the wild.

A career counselor was dumbstruck by Jane's descriptions of her future aspirations. She thought it was bizarre that a young girl would want to work so intimately with wild animals in Africa. Her advice to Jane was that she study photography. That way she could take portraits of people's pet dogs, and she would be able to work with animals. Jane flatly rejected that idea. The only people who believed in Jane were her family, and when the counselor gave such a disappointing suggestion, Jane turned to her mother for advice.

Jane has often said in interviews and writings about Vanne that "her whole philosophy to me, all through my childhood was, if you really want something, you work hard, you take advantage of opportunity and you never give up. You will find a way." With this reasoning, Vanne convinced her daughter that she should train to be a secretary. After all, secretaries could travel anywhere in the world, and maybe Jane could find a way to travel to Africa. So at nineteen, in May 1953, Jane moved to London to begin her training, studying typing, shorthand, and bookkeeping at Queen's Secretarial College in South Kensington, and living in a rented room in the home of a family friend.

Though she now lived in a city, Jane found a way to be around animals as often as possible. On weekends she sometimes headed home to Bournemouth in Uncle Eric's car or by train. Other weekends she visited family friends, the Seabrooks, at their farm in Kent. Jane became fast friends with the Seabrooks' daughter, Jo, and they spent much of their time riding horses in the country.

On March 6, 1954, Jane completed her secretarial schooling. She could type 51 words per minute and write shorthand at 110 words per minute. She received very high grades and, within a few months, found a job at the Oxford University Registry. Though the job did not involve animals, her supervisor allowed Jane to bring her pet hamster, Hamlette, to the office.

Living in Oxford was exciting for Jane. The city was home to Oxford University, so being there as a secretary had all the social benefits of being a student but none of the schoolwork. Her job was a different story. Jane did not enjoy being a secretary—in a 1955 letter, she told her mother and grandmother that "I want to write about . . . this vile job. . . . I have been miserable these last few weeks because of the boredom of this foul job, but now the thought of future jobs perks me up no end." She confessed to friends that she had not given up on becoming a journalist or writer. She justified her interlude as a secretary as an opportunity to experience life in order to write more meaningful pieces.

In April 1955, a family friend, Alvar Lidell, arranged an interview for Jane for a position at a commercial film studio in London, Stanley Schofield Productions. Jane got the job, which involved doing a bit of everything from entertaining customers to editing film. By June she was living in her father's apartment in London. Jane found life in London even more exciting than Oxford had been. She spent hours visiting museums and art galleries, and attending classical music concerts. She also flirted with young men whom she met, which created a full and active social life. These flirtations had an additional advantage—as Jane remembered, "In those days if a man invited a girl to go out with him, he would have been horrified if she had tried to pay her share. This helped a lot, as I was desperately short of money; it meant that when I was taken out to dinner I could do without lunch."

While Jane enjoyed London, it was far from the African wilderness she still dreamed of. She worried that working at a place such as Schofield would never help her realize that dream. But quite unexpectedly, a door to Africa cracked open. Jane received a letter from an old friend from the Uplands Girls School, Marie Claude Mange, known as Clo. Clo's letter came with two stamps, one with an elephant on it and another with two giraffes on it. Jane immediately realized that the letter was from Africa.

In her letter, Clo informed Jane that her parents had bought a farm in Kenya, and she invited Jane for a visit. Jane wanted to quit her job on the spot and accept the offer, but Vanne wanted her to make sure that the invitation was serious.

Jane received confirmation from Clo in May 1956, but she could not rush off to Africa right away—she did not have the $670 for a round-trip ticket. Jane had to save money, so she gave notice to Schofield that she was leaving and moved back to Bournemouth to find a new job. Since she would not pay living expenses while staying at home, her entire salary could be saved for the trip to Africa.

Jane found a job as a waitress at a nearby hotel restaurant, and she worked through the day, serving all of the meals and two afternoon teas. She only had one day off every two weeks. She became an expert waitress and could carry up to thirteen plates at the same time without a tray.

Every weekend, Jane put each coin that she had earned under the carpet in the drawing room of the Birches. After five months of working and saving, Jane had the entire family gather in the drawing room, and closed the curtains for privacy. She then took out her savings and counted the money. She had finally saved enough. She remembered thinking at the time, "I could go to Africa—and my life would be changed forever."

Jane poses with a stuffed monkey, 1962.

Two

ON WEDNESDAY, March 13, 1957, at the age of twenty-two, Jane boarded the *Kenya Castle*, the ship that would take her from London to Africa. The trip took three weeks, and in that time Jane shared a cabin with four other girls. Jane took a dislike to one of the girls, nicknaming her Old Fur Coat, but she became fast friends with the others.

The journey took her southward past the equator, down the western coast of Africa, around the Cape of Good Hope, and finally up to Kenya. During the trip, Jane wrote to her family: "I <u>still</u> find it difficult to believe that I am on my way to <u>Africa</u>. That is the thing—AFRICA. It is easy to imagine I am going for a long sea voyage, but not that names like Mombasa, Nairobi, South Kinangop, Nakuru, etc., are going to become reality."

Finally, the ship docked in Mombasa, Kenya, on April 2, and Jane disembarked and began a two-day train ride to Nairobi. Clo and her family were waiting at the train station for Jane when she arrived late on April 3, her twenty-third birthday.

During the drive to the farm in Kinangop, along a dirt road that climbed up the South Kinangop Highlands, Jane had her first glimpse of some of the animals she had only read about in books. A lone male giraffe stood by the side of the road before gracefully cantering away. The car braked hard to avoid hitting an aardvark that had wandered into the road.

In the next few weeks, Jane became familiar with the sounds of African birds and the tracks of animals such as leopards. She said that "it was all so new and exciting and beautiful."

Jane did not want to take advantage of the Manges' hospitality interminably. Even before she left England, she had made arrangements to find work as a secretary to support herself while she explored Africa. After a few weeks with the Manges, Jane headed back to Nairobi to start working. Though Jane considered the job boring, it gave her enough money to get by until she could find some other employment. Hopefully she would be able to find something that would allow her to work with animals.

After a dinner party one night, someone suggested to Jane that if she really wanted to learn about animals, she should contact Louis Leakey. Louis was a famous anthropologist and paleontologist at the Coryndon Museum in Nairobi. He had a vast knowledge of African people and animals—in fact, Louis had grown up among the members of the African Kikuyu tribe, with whom his father worked as a missionary. Louis was involved in several research projects studying the origins of some African animals and the behavior of others.

Jane made an appointment for ten o'clock on May 24 with Louis. When she arrived, Louis personally took her around the museum and asked her many questions about the exhibits. Jane had read so much about Africa that she answered most of his questions correctly. She remembered that she "apparently enchanted him too with [her] youthful enthusiasm, [her] love for animals, and [her] determination to get to Africa."

By the time Jane met Louis, the esteemed scientist

was white haired and gray mustached, and had developed a habit of wearing one-piece khaki overalls with missing buttons and overflowing pockets. He smoked cigars and did not bathe often, meaning that he tended to stink—but he was enthusiastic about his work and generous with his knowledge.

Since his previous secretary had just left, Louis offered Jane that job starting in September. She eagerly agreed. It was the perfect opportunity to learn about East African animals directly from the museum. She also could learn a great deal from Louis himself. She said later, "Here was the whole panorama of life in Africa laid out between the walls of one building. And it was a feast for me to see all these things. But they were dead and they were stuffed, and I didn't like that." Jane considered the museum job only a first step toward her goal of working with real African animals.

Every year, Louis and his second wife, Mary, traveled to Olduvai Gorge on the Serengeti Plain to look for fossils, especially those from the ancestors of humans. Louis invited Jane to join him on their trip that August. Mary agreed to the arrangement so long as another

English woman who worked at the museum, Gillian Trace, would come as well. Jane did not fully realize it at the time, but Louis was known to have a roving eye, and Mary may have suspected that Louis was interested in the young and beautiful Jane for more than just her mind. Jane, however, made the trip arrangements while blissfully unaware of Louis's reputation.

Though Olduvai Gorge lies in the eastern part of the Serengeti Plain, in present-day Tanzania, the area was largely unknown in 1957 since the Serengeti was not yet a major tourist destination. There was no formal road or track leading into Olduvai, because it was so remote. To get there, researchers traveled over wild, grassy lands in sturdy vehicles, while the wild animals that lived in the Serengeti looked on.

Olduvai Gorge is made up of two irregular ravines—a main one that is twenty-five miles long and three hundred feet deep and a second fifteen-mile-long one that intersects the first. Louis, having grown up in Africa, became interested in the fossils at Olduvai as a student at Cambridge University. By 1957 he had been digging there for his own research for almost two decades.

Going to Olduvai would be unlike anything Jane had ever experienced. All food and drink had to be brought in, so Louis inquired whether there were foods that Jane could not eat or particularly disliked. In addition, water would be scarce. Each member of the expedition would only get a small bowl of water daily for washing and a limited amount of water for a once-weekly bath in a canvas tub. Jane wrote, "It was a real expedition into the 'wilds of Africa,' such as I had dreamed of since childhood."

Jane weighed the lack of water carefully with respect to one particular issue—the state of her hair. Jane's hair was long, and she worried that it would get very dirty and greasy in Olduvai. She considered cutting it short but thought that would lead to her hair looking stringy. Instead, she settled on pulling it back into a ponytail. The blonde, ponytailed woman working and living in the wildest parts of the world would become Jane's trademark look.

On July 15, Jane and Gillian sat on the roof of the over-packed Land Rover in which the Leakeys traveled as the group approached Olduvai from Ngorongoro. Their job was to look out for the faint tire tracks from the previous year's journey to Olduvai. The group arrived at sunset and quickly set up their tents.

During the stay at Olduvai, Jane encountered miniature antelopes called dik-diks, small herds of Grant's gazelles, and, occasionally, giraffes. Once she was confronted by a black rhino. The great beast sensed her presence and snorted and pawed at the ground before turning to leave. On another occasion, Jane and Gillian felt that they were being watched—and turned to see a young lion gazing at them from forty feet away. He softly growled to warn them not to come any closer; the young women heeded the warning. In the evenings, from her bed inside the camp tent, Jane could hear the distant roars of lions and the giggling sounds and catlike yowls of hyenas. She said, "It was wild, untouched Africa. There were all the animals of my childhood dreams. So that I woke up every morning in my dream. I was there."

Most of Jane's time at the gorge was spent digging for fossils beneath the glare of the hot African sun. She worked side by side with Mary and members of the Kenyan staff. First, each site was prepared for excavation by the Kenyan staff. They cleared the topsoil and upper layers to expose the fossil bed beneath. Next, Mary and Jane began excavating, a task that took hours of often monotonous and repetitive actions. In the fossil bed, the women used hunting knives to chip through the hard soil until they got close to something interesting. At that point, they switched to dental picks to protect the fossils. They worked for eight hours every day, with a break at eleven o'clock for coffee and a three-hour break in the middle of the day to avoid working in the hottest hours.

Louis and Mary hoped to find fossil evidence of ancestors of humans, but the work was slow and tedious, and often all that was found after a day of toil was as mundane as mouse bones. Jane wrote to her family in Bournemouth, "The great aim here is to find the man who made all the tools—primitive pebble tools & the beginnings of the more evolved hand axe. So far 2 teeth have been found—2 years ago. The day before yesterday . . . there was great excitement because I found what could—and still may—be a human tooth. LSB is not sure yet. It might be a female baboon." Jane added that she hoped that when human fossils were found, Louis would be the one to find them, since "he is so sweet, so utterly adorable. . . . With his grey hair tousled & falling over his forehead & his grey eyes twinkling, he looks for all the world like a naughty little boy."

In the weeks she spent at Olduvai, Jane grew to like Louis a great deal. She also talked to him at length about the great apes—which include chimpanzees, gorillas, and orangutans. He had heard of several sightings of the eastern, or long-haired, variety of chimpanzees about six hundred miles southwest of Olduvai, near the port city of Kigoma on the northeastern shore of Lake Tanganyika. He wanted to begin a scientific study of these chimps, focusing on their behavior. Since these animals are the closest living relatives of humans, Louis believed that studying them would help people better understand ancient human ancestors.

Louis's proposed project wouldn't be simple. There were no guidelines for that kind of scientific study on chimps since no one had ever done it before. In addition, the researcher would have to live in a remote and rough area among wild and dangerous animals. At the time of their discussion, Jane couldn't imagine whom Louis would find to take on such a difficult assignment.

ഌൟഌൟ

The conversation between Louis and Jane about the chimps took place near the end of the summer in Olduvai. In September, it was time to return to Nairobi. There, Jane indulged her love of animals by amassing a personal collection of strays that needed a home. The first was a lesser bush baby called Levi. During the day, Jane brought him to Louis's office at the museum, where Levi slept inside a large gourd. He surprised many of Louis's visitors by awaking when he heard the sound of a strange voice and leaping from the gourd onto the visitor's shoulders. At night, Levi caught and ate insects.

Next, Jane acquired Kobi, a vervet monkey, and Kip, a dwarf mongoose. Soon after, there was a wife for Kobi, called Lettuce, and one for Kip, called Mrs. Kip, then a hedgehog, a rat, a cocker spaniel called Tana, a springer spaniel called Hobo, a Siamese cat called Nanky-Poo, and a greater bush baby called Boozy.

Despite her pets, Jane was still preoccupied with thoughts of other animals. She couldn't get the chimpanzee project out of her mind—though that did not stop her from focusing on romance. In the summer of

1957, Jane had met Brian Herne, the son of a camp manager at Ngorongoro. Brian worked as a guide for tourists on hunting expeditions. When the couple first met, Brian was recovering from a car accident; both of his legs were in casts from his waist to his toes, and he came across as very brave to Jane.

Jane wrote to her family that "when I got him on his own . . . I began to realize that the character underneath . . . is one of the very nicest I've come across out here. . . . Brian was only supposed to be in Nairobi for 10 days. He stayed 3 weeks or more— because of yours truly." Jane later admitted that her relationship with Brian was her first real love affair. It was exciting, though a bit stormy. When Vanne met Brian eventually, she thought that he was charming but somewhat melodramatic.

Jane's social life encompassed more than just her ongoing relationship with Brian. In late 1957, her relationship with Louis had become complicated. Her mentor was indeed interested in a romance with Jane. Once Louis tried to convince Jane to meet him for an overnight camping trip in nearby Tsavo National Park. Another time, Jane was resting in her room when suddenly there was a loud knocking on her door. When she opened it, Louis's hand appeared holding a red rose, which was, as Jane described, "a token of his love." Jane wrote to Vanne and Danny: "My situation here is really getting more and more tricky every day. Old Louis really is infantile in his infatuation and is suggesting the most impossible things. I have absolutely no intention of getting involved with him in the ways he suggests."

Louis was not the only middle-aged man to vie for Jane's affections. She was young, pretty, and extroverted, and enjoyed attention—she tended to flirt. Many of the men who fell for Jane were easily avoided, but Louis was a different story. Jane saw him every day and worked closely with him. She was not worried, though. She trusted Louis and had every confidence that he would respect her wishes to keep their relationship professional. At the same time, she worried about her reputation if others—especially Louis's wife—caught wind of his interest. Jane was not willing to leave her job, though. She was still enjoying her work at the museum, and Louis still had much to teach her. She simply decided to prevent any inappropriate behavior.

ഇ ങ ഇ ങ

After another few months of working at the museum, Jane had saved enough money to buy a plane ticket to Kenya for Vanne. She wrote, "All my life, up to that time, she had been doing things for me. Now, at last, I could do something for her." On September 2, 1958, Vanne boarded a plane in London and arrived in Nairobi the following day for an extended three-month visit with her daughter.

Vanne moved into Jane's apartment. She loved Africa, and Jane loved having her nearby. Louis arranged for Vanne to see a great deal of Africa's natural wonders, including organizing a trip to Olduvai. In addition, as a special treat, Louis arranged for Vanne and Jane to spend a weekend on his research boat, the *Miocene Lady*, sailing on the second-largest freshwater lake in the world, Lake Victoria. Jane and Vanne spent a day exploring Lolui, an island in Lake Victoria filled with monkeys and other wildlife.

During Vanne's stay, mother and daughter talked about Jane's future. Vanne was still supportive of Jane's dream to study animals in nature, but being Louis's assistant wasn't providing the opportunities that Jane had hoped for. Jane's plan was to return to England with her mother within a few weeks because it was not clear how she could find a job working with animals in Africa.

Louis repeatedly talked to Jane about the work he wanted done with chimpanzees. Jane could hardly bear to listen, as Louis was describing her dream job. One day, she blurted out that admission, and Louis's response stunned her. He said, "I've been waiting for you to tell me that. Why on earth did you think I talked about those chimpanzees to you?"

Jane was astonished that Louis would consider her as a candidate for this study. She did not have a degree from a university or any formal training. And she was a woman—in 1957, it was almost unheard of to think of a woman living alone in the bush. Louis, however, did not mind that Jane did not have formal credentials. In fact, he preferred for the researcher for the project to go into it with an open mind, unbiased by the conventions of the scientific world. Louis wanted someone who would be patient and hardworking, who loved animals, and who would be able to live away from civilization for a long time, possibly several years. As Jane remembered, "When he put it like that, of course, I had to admit I was the perfect choice!"

Jane was eager to head into the bush to begin the study, but there were several hurdles to overcome first. Louis had to get governmental approval from Tanganyika, and he had to find funding for the project. He had already obtained necessary governmental permission for a young woman to study the chimpanzees at the Gombe Stream Chimpanzee Reserve, but she could not go alone. The expedition needed an official second member, someone who would act as Jane's companion and assistant. Louis mentioned this to Vanne, and she saw an opportunity to aid in Jane's dreams. She immediately volunteered to join the expedition, even though she later admitted that she had no idea what possessed her to do so.

Unfortunately, Louis had not found a financial sponsor yet, and there was no way to know how long that would take or if he would even find someone willing to sponsor Jane's project. There was nothing for the women to do in Africa until the funds were secured. Therefore, Jane and Vanne decided to return to

England as scheduled, and Jane would begin to train in zoology while she waited.

Jane knew that if she did return to Africa, it would not be to Nairobi and the Coryndon Museum. This meant that she had to decide what to do about Brian. Because of their relationship, his profession as a hunter posed a problem to Jane. As she explained, "He hunted and he killed the very animals I had come to Africa to live with and learn about. In my youthful naïveté, I suppose I thought I could change him. Of course I couldn't." Overall, Jane did not feel that the relationship could survive separation, and she and Brian decided to end things. So Jane left Africa, hoping the separation would only be temporary.

Three

IN JANUARY 1959, Jane moved back into her father's apartment in London. Her sister, Judy, also lived there, studying piano at the Guildhall School of Music & Drama. Jane began to prepare for the chimpanzee study by reading and scrutinizing reports from primate studies that had already been completed. She still needed a job to make ends meet, so she began working at the film library of Granada Television at the London Zoo as the assistant to the librarian. She was quite memorable to her coworkers since she came to work with Kip and Boozy. Both of Jane's pets were eventually featured in films produced by the zoo.

While Jane ticked off the months in London, Louis kept trying to arrange the details of the chimp study. He was unable to find a traditional source of funding for the project, and so he turned to his friend Leighton Wilkie, a wealthy American who had created a philanthropic organization called the Wilkie Brothers Foundation. Wilkie already funded some of Louis's work in Olduvai, so Louis proposed that his foundation award him a second grant to underwrite his chimpanzee project. Louis's proposal mentioned Miss Jane Morris-Goodall as the researcher of choice—though Louis conveniently omitted Jane's background as a secretary. Instead, he described her as being one of his coworkers in Kenya. He also told them that Jane was doing further research in London until the grant was awarded.

Wilkie was enthusiastic about the project and offered Louis three thousand dollars for the research. On a brief stop in London in December 1959 on his way back to Kenya from the United States, Louis told Jane about the grant and that the chimpanzee project would certainly happen. But it was still not clear when Jane would start. Her life in London was going quite well, and that fall twenty-five-year-old Jane had met a twenty-six-year-old actor named Robert Young. Jane

Jane wearing her standard field uniform.

called him Bob. The two were immediately attracted to each other and began a relationship.

Bob admired that Jane was ambitious and knew what she wanted to do with her life. Within a few months, early in 1960, Bob asked Jane's father if he could marry his daughter. Jane's father was caught completely off guard, and to Bob's amusement, asked him which one.

Despite the awkward start, Mortimer and Bob settled into a happy conversation, and Jane and Bob went on to become officially engaged. She was concerned about how her plans to go back to Africa would work with Bob's career, but she reasoned that she would only go back to Africa for a few months to study the chimpanzees and then return to England. Bob wanted to get married before Jane returned to Africa, but she resisted because, as she wrote in March 1960, "First I have got to find out whether I can live without Africa."

On May 13, 1960, Jane and Bob's engagement was announced in the *Daily Telegram & Morning Post*. The couple barely had a chance to enjoy the engagement, though. Louis had finalized the arrangements for the study at long last, and on May 31, Jane and Vanne left for Nairobi. Through a haze of tears, Jane and Bob consoled themselves that the separation would be short lived.

Bad news awaited Jane and Vanne's arrival in Nairobi the following day—there would be another delay. Some of the fishermen who camped in the area around the chimpanzee reserve were disputing fishing rights, making the entire area unsafe. Jane remembered feeling disappointed, but "luckily for my peace of mind Louis [Leakey] immediately put forward the suggestion that I should make a short trial study of the vervet monkeys on an island in Lake Victoria." So instead of waiting for the dispute to be settled, on June 11, 1960, Jane and Vanne went to Lolui island, the same one they had visited on Vanne's last trip to Africa. The vervet monkey study would serve as a trial run for the chimp study.

Jane began taking notes on the monkeys in the field immediately. The notes themselves were part of the learning experience—after all, there were no guidelines for Jane to follow. Her approach to studying the monkeys, largely based on instinct, was the one she would later employ to study chimpanzees. Instead of stalking the animals like a predator or hunter, Jane, to a certain extent, repeated what she had done years ago on Danny Nutt's farm when she wanted to learn about hens and laying. She openly, though carefully, approached the monkeys, respecting their boundaries and only getting as close as they were comfortable with.

During the time Jane spent on Lolui, she woke up around five forty-five in the morning. To make sure she was there when the monkeys woke up, Jane didn't even bother to eat anything before she left the boat for the island. The captain of the *Miocene Lady*, Hassan Salimu, rowed her to shore, and she waited in the grass for the monkeys to begin stirring. Jane remained in the field until around nine A.M., when she returned to the deck of the boat to eat breakfast with Vanne. Afterward, mother and daughter headed back to Lolui. Jane settled in to watch the monkeys again, and Vanne busied herself collecting specimens of the island's insects and vegetation.

Jane would linger on the island until after sunset, when the monkeys had returned to their trees to sleep. Vanne, on the other hand, would return to the *Miocene Lady* for most of the afternoon, meeting with her daughter for supper after the daylight had faded and Jane could no longer see the monkeys. Back on the boat, Jane wrote up her notes for the day. Every night at nine o'clock faithfully, she listened to the news on the radio, since Louis was planning to send a safari message via the news program when he wanted Jane and Vanne to return to Nairobi. The radio was the only way for Louis to contact Jane quickly.

Day after day, Jane sat almost motionless, watching and waiting, staring and studying. "At that time," Jane remembered, "my fears of being harmed by a wild animal were almost nonexistent. I truly believed that the animals would sense that I intended no harm and, in turn, would leave me alone." Vanne saw that her daughter was utterly dedicated to the work and happier than she had ever been. Jane recorded every behavioral aspect of the monkeys she could observe, making distinctions among individuals and their unique features and personalities. As soon as she could tell one from another, Jane gave the monkeys names that she used in her field notes. This was an unusual way to approach the research, as other scientists did not personalize their animal subjects. Jane had no scientific training at this point, though, so she did not even realize that she might be doing things differently.

Louis's safari message finally came on June 25, and Jane and Vanne left Lolui on June 29. Jane gave Louis her report on the vervet monkey study; he read and sighed a great deal but in the end seemed happy with Jane's work.

On Tuesday, July 5, the Land Rover was packed for the trip to Gombe with supplies such as tents, chairs, mosquito netting, boxes of food, water bottles, and haversacks. Jane and Vanne waved good-bye to Louis and the museum staff, while Bernard Verdcourt, a botanist at the Coryndon Museum, took the wheel to drive them to Kigoma, the nearest port city to Gombe. After three days and one emergency brake repair, Jane, Vanne, and Verdcourt arrived at the edge of Lake Tanganyika at sunset. The view of the blue water and the steel-colored mountains was breathtaking. The following day, Saturday, they arrived in Kigoma.

The first order of business was to check in with the district commissioner in Kigoma to notify him of Jane's arrival and that she would be off to Gombe immediately. The government offices were closed on Saturdays, but Jane and Vanne managed to track him down. Unfortunately, he gave the women more bad news about their expedition—across the lake, in the newly independent country of the Republic of Congo, political strife and violence were leading Congolese refugees to cross Lake Tanganyika into Kigoma. As Jane remembered, "He explained, regretfully but firmly, that there was no chance at all of my proceeding to the chimpanzee reserve. First it was necessary to find out how the local Kigoma district Africans would react to the tales of rioting and disorder in the Congo." The commissioner feared that the violence would spread into the area where Jane and Vanne were planning to settle. Jane would have to wait again.

Verdcourt checked the three of them into individual rooms at a hotel, but soon the hotel was teeming with refugees, and there wasn't enough space available to keep single rooms. Jane and Vanne moved into the same room, cramming themselves into the little bit of space left over after their supplies were stored. Jane, Vanne, and Verdcourt offered to help the residents of Kigoma and the refugees in any way they could. They handed out fruit, cigarettes, chocolate, and beer, and one night they helped assemble two thousand SPAM sandwiches. Jane wrote, "I have never been able to face tinned spam from that day to this."

Finally, on July 14, the official permission for Jane to go to Gombe was granted. Jane and Vanne bid farewell to Verdcourt, and the two women, as well as their newly hired cook, Dominic Charles Bandora, headed to the chimpanzee reserve. The supplies were packed onto a Tanganyika Game Department launch boat, the *Kibisi*, and they journeyed across the lake for the two-hour trip.

Jane remembered thinking that surely some other catastrophe would occur to prevent her from reaching Gombe—perhaps the boat would sink or she would fall overboard and be eaten by a crocodile—but her luck was changing. It took about an hour before the banks of Gombe came into view, and the *Kibisi* dropped anchor at Kasekela village, home to several local Africans and headquarters of two government game scouts. Jane, Vanne, and Bandora, with some help from the local children, set up on the beach.

Jane and Vanne shared a large tent that held two cots and included a separate washroom and a raised-flap veranda. They placed mosquito netting over the entire front of the tent and fashioned a decent latrine, a deep hole in the ground surrounded by a makeshift fence of woven palm leaves.

That evening, one of the game scouts, Adolf Siwezi, alerted Jane that a chimpanzee had been sighted. Jane and Siwezi hurried to the spot and found a dark ape obscured by leaves and other vegetation. They tried to approach the animal, but the chimp retreated deeper into the forest.

Four

THE GOMBE STREAM Chimpanzee Reserve (now called the Gombe Stream National Park) is a stretch of land on the northeastern shore of Lake Tanganyika about ten miles long. One side of the reserve is bounded by the rocky shoreline and the other by a steep, 2,500-foot-high cliff. Approximately fifteen streams tumble from the reserve down to the lake shore; Gombe Stream itself is only one of these.

The land is a rugged rectangle inhabited by many types of animals, including chimps, olive baboons, several varieties of monkeys, bush babies, civets, genets, bushbucks, leopards, bush pigs, and a wide assortment of poisonous snakes. Jane remembered thinking, "What had I, the girl standing on the government launch in her jeans, to do with the girl who, in a few days, would be searching those

Jane with David Greybeard in her camp at Gombe, 1965.

very mountains for wild chimpanzees?" Jane came to
Gombe without the pedigree of most scientists but
with something that would prove to be much more
important—an open mind.

When the study began, Jane was clearly the lead
researcher. Vanne had no role in the research, and instead she befriended the local villagers and fishermen

by opening a small clinic. Jane wrote, "How lucky I was to have a mother like Vanne—a mother in a million. I could not have done without her during those early days." Even though Vanne was not with Jane in the wild, she was not on her own. The government required that one of the game scouts, Siwezi, accompany her at all times. In addition, the government officials insisted that Jane hire a porter to carry her belongings on her daily hikes. Jane hired Rashidi Kikwale for that job. Siwezi was paid by the Tanganyikan government, but Jane herself had to pay Kikwale two shillings a day.

Jane was disheartened that she would not be free to move about on her own. She strongly felt that the chimps would be comfortable with her only if she approached them alone. But she realized that she had no choice in the matter and reluctantly agreed.

On her third full day there, July 17, 1960, at eight thirty in the morning, Jane, Siwezi, and Kikwale heard the cries of several chimps and spotted them feeding in a *msulula* tree, picking the red and orange berries off by hand and eating them. They found a spot on a hillside that was high enough for Jane to watch the approximately ten chimps through her binoculars but far enough not to disturb them.

Over the first week, Jane watched the chimps from morning until night. She even slept out in the forest on occasion so that she would be able to observe the animals the moment they awoke. But Jane was frustrated by the distance and the trees that obscured her line of sight.

By late July, a new frustration surfaced. Siwezi and Kikwale did not share Jane's passion for studying chimpanzees, so they were unwilling to wake up early and became tired much more easily than Jane did. Jane walked from dawn until dusk, searching for good vantage points from which to view the chimps and often searching for the chimps themselves. By the end of each day of following her, her companions were on the verge of mutiny. Even though she had promised to always be accompanied by Siwezi and Kikwale, Jane often went off on her own rather that wait for the unenthusiastic men. By September 1, an old friend of Jane's from her Nairobi days, Derrick Dunn, a farmer and white hunter, had made arrangements for two of his best safari trackers to go to Gombe to replace Siwezi and Kikwale. The new arrivals made it easier for Jane to cover the distances she wanted to in a day, though few people could match Jane's stamina.

When Louis secured funding for the chimpanzee project from the Wilkie Brothers Foundation, he had proposed an approximately four-month study to end on December 1, 1960. As summer progressed, the chimpanzees did not cooperate with that timeline. For many long, depressing weeks, Jane walked for hours every day and barely observed any animals. She wrote, "In between the disappointing days when we only saw chimps too far off to observe properly or, for a few minutes, close by, before they fled, were even worse days when we saw no chimps at all." Whenever she encountered a chimp, the animal scurried away before Jane caught more than a glimpse of dark hair. It was easy for Jane's spirits to fall in light of her lack of success.

The one positive thing was that Jane grew accustomed to life at the reserve. Her skin toughened against the rough vegetation. Her body grew immune to tsetse fly bites so that she no longer swelled when bitten. She grew familiar with the geography and terrain, and could travel through the forest more sure-footedly.

But on August 16, 1960, Jane had a breakthrough. As she watched over an open area from a high point where she had perched herself, an older chimpanzee with a white beard approached her, coming within ten yards. As Jane described in her field journal: "His expression was one of amazement. He stopped abruptly. Stared. Put his head on one side & then on the other, and then turned & cantered off into the thicker undergrowth." A few days later, Jane spotted another white-bearded older male, and wondered if it was the same chimp.

Gradually, the chimpanzees seemed to become aware of Jane's presence. She decided that she would act as much like another primate as she could. She scratched herself, looked for insects, dug in the ground with her hands, and pretended to eat. Instead of staring directly at the chimps, which seemed to disturb them, she pretended that she was not at all interested in them. The chimps, on the other hand, often stared directly at Jane. By September, they seemed to have begun to accept Jane, at least on some occasions. On September 16, Jane wrote that the white-bearded male, which she eventually named David Greybeard, sat fifteen yards away from her with "absolutely no fear."

Jane recorded as much information about the chimps as she could, describing their physical appearance, the sounds they made, and the way they moved. In addition, she described what they ate—even going so far as to taste whatever she could. She also collected dung specimens to learn more about the chimps' diet.

Jane discovered that young chimpanzees were capable of what she considered imaginative play, such as tickling each other for the joy of it and playing with a tall, thick branch as if it was a piece of playground equipment. She also discovered that chimpanzee mothers had what she felt were very close and loving relationships with their children. Mothers cradled their young and nursed their babies, in Jane's words, "in exactly human fashion." In the evenings, Jane observed the chimpanzees constructing nests in the branches of trees to sleep in, and she tested one of these night nests herself by climbing up into it and stretching out.

She wrote, "I found that there was quite complicated interweaving of the branches in some of them . . . [and] that the nests were never fouled with dung."

As Jane continued observing, she began to be able to distinguish one chimp from another. By September 12, she had begun to give the chimps names. Jane later wrote, "People often ask me how I choose such names for individual chimpanzees. My answer is that some names—such as Mrs. Maggs, Spray, and Mr. McGregor—simply come to mind. Strange as it may sound, some chimpanzees remind me of friends or acquaintances in some gesture or manner and are named accordingly." Sophie was an ugly female whose son was Sophocles. Flo was an older female with a deformed, bulbous nose and ragged ears; her son and daughter, Figan and Fifi, were constantly with her. Claud was bearded and had a grizzled appearance, and Annie was a bold older female. And, of course, David Greybeard was the older male with a distinctive gray beard.

In October, Jane and Vanne hosted a scientist named George Schaller and his wife, Kay. Schaller had made a name for himself by doing a study on gorillas in East Africa that was similar to Jane's. He had managed to put the gorillas at ease to observe their behaviors closely. Jane knew that he would be able to provide her with priceless advice on her own work with the chimpanzees, and she looked forward to spending time with him.

Schaller was appalled that Jane had so little equipment, and that Louis had only planned for a four-month study. He suggested that a small grant would provide the money to get better equipment and to stay longer, which would yield more significant results. Jane listened eagerly to Schaller's suggestions. She was upset that her study was coming to an end and worried that Louis would be disappointed by the small amount she had learned. Schaller was a sympathetic ear and one of the few people on Earth who could truly understand what Jane was trying to do.

Schaller's most important contribution to Jane's study may have been that he helped her identify a goal. As Jane wrote: "George said he thought that if I could see chimps eating meat, or using a tool, a whole year's work would be justified." At the time, it was believed that chimps didn't do either of these things, so observing either behavior would be a breakthrough and would challenge the scientific world's perceptions about chimpanzees.

Schaller's comment made Jane look more carefully for any signs of meat eating by the chimps. And on October 30, Jane's diligence was rewarded. That morning, she witnessed three chimps screaming angrily and holding something that appeared to be pink. As she watched, it became clear that the pink object was meat, and she watched the chimps bite and suck on it. On later occasions, Jane observed chimps acting as predators, killing other animals with their hands and teeth and then feeding on their kills.

A few days after observing the meat eating, Jane achieved Schaller's other goal—observing the chimps using tools. On November 6, as Jane trekked through the forest, she recognized David Greybeard about sixty yards away. She carefully positioned herself so she could watch what David was doing. She saw him take a piece of straw and poke it into a tunnel in the termite mound. He removed it a few moments later, and Jane saw that the straw was covered in termites. David swiped the straw through his lips and ate the insects.

When the straw got bent, David stripped the leaves off a twig and used that instead.

In her notes, Jane described David's actions as termite fishing. Over the next eight days, she kept a vigil near the termite mound to try to catch another sighting of termite fishing. On the eighth day she was rewarded with the sight of David and another chimp repeating the fishing expedition over the course of two hours. Jane wrote that "on several occasions they picked little leafy twigs and prepared them for use by stripping off the leaves. This was the first recorded example of a wild animal not merely *using* an object as a tool, but actually modifying an object and thus showing the crude beginnings of tool-*making*." This was a significant step for Jane's research, and for Jane personally—after all, she was the first person to witness a chimp making a tool.

Jane telegrammed Louis about the meat eating and tool making, and he was equally pleased by Jane's observations. Making and using tools was one way that scientists had traditionally defined humans as being different from animals. He immediately wrote to Jane: "Now we must redefine 'tool,' redefine 'man,' or accept chimpanzees as human."

In light of her breakthroughs, Louis, whom Jane had begun to call Fairy Foster Father or FFF, told her that she would have to make new plans for her future. In true fairy form, he began to open doors for her to help her create the life she wanted—a life spent studying wild chimpanzees. First, Louis decided to enroll Jane at Cambridge University to get a PhD, the highest scientific degree available, even though Jane did not have an undergraduate degree. A PhD would give Jane more clout in the scientific community and allow her research to be taken seriously, so Louis was determined to make this happen. Second, he began looking for funding to extend Jane's study (picking up the tab himself in the interim).

Jane decided to remain in Africa until the end of the chimpanzee termite-fishing season the following December, in 1961. After that, she planned to head back to England to begin studying at Cambridge, but only temporarily. She already knew that the bulk of her time over the next few years would be spent in Gombe. In light of these plans, Jane ended her engagement to Bob Young. He wrote that he respected her decision while being very disappointed by the news. Jane hardly had time to look back, however, since there were too many possibilities on the horizon.

On December 1, 1960, Jane left Gombe with her friend Derrick Dunn to go on a short safari. The safari trackers who had been hired to accompany Jane at Gombe left when she did, and Jane decided that she was not going to hire replacements. She felt comfortable enough at Gombe that she no longer needed professional scouts. The requirement that Jane have a companion had been forgotten by the authorities in Kigoma. They had grown comfortable with Jane living at Gombe and did not worry about a chaperone any longer. She wrote, "I was, by then, part of the Gombe Stream landscape." Jane was not alone, though, since she had her camp staff, Hassan Salimu, the captain of the *Miocene Lady*; Bandora; his wife Chiko and daughter Ado; as well as Kikwale, who had returned.

After the safari, Jane spent the weeks around Christmas in Nairobi, visiting Louis and other friends. When she returned to Gombe on January 14, 1961, she went back alone. Vanne had left for home the previous November, as she was scheduled to do from the beginning. Though Vanne was no longer in Africa, Jane kept in constant touch with her—and all the women at the Birches—through letters.

Jane's second stint at Gombe was different from her first. On February 6, she wrote to her family, "I now climb the mountains on my own. . . . So my mountain climbing cloths [sic] are now practical, if slightly unconventional. I tie my trousers round my waist, & my polythene sheet around my waist too, & there I am. The top half doesn't get too wet. Occasionally, if I am forced to walk about in the rain, I bare that to the elements as well!!" Because Jane walked through the forest alone, it was possible to work half naked—but the unusual dress code didn't change the nature of the work. Every day was physically difficult. Aside from the great distances Jane hiked and the harsh and wet weather conditions, there were other challenges to working at Gombe. Extreme humidity caused a white, funguslike growth between Jane's toes and under all of her toenails. She had fevers and headaches. Still, Jane persevered with calm and attentiveness, and her hard work was rewarded with new breakthroughs.

On January 31, she witnessed the most exciting

event she had seen yet. She had come upon a large group of chimps, and at first the children were wildly frolicking up in the trees. Suddenly, they disappeared, and Jane redirected her attention to the six adults—five males and one female—that were quietly feeding in the trees. Soon, they all climbed down from their various perches and then climbed up a single tree. After a few moments, the children reappeared, along with two new adults, and the chidlren began to play silently but vigorously for about an hour. At that point it began to rain. Jane thought the apes would go find shelter, as she had observed them doing on other rainy days. Instead, they climbed down from the tree and gathered in two groups about 150 feet apart from each other. The groups were moving in parallel, single-file processions up the hill when one of the adult males left his group and ran full speed toward the other group while making calling sounds. Jane thought the display was impressive. When the chimps reached the top of the hill, they climbed trees and the Rain Festival, as Jane called it, began. The adult males jumped down from their perches, sometimes ripping off large branches from the trees and charging down the hill.

Jane wrote to her family, "Mostly the actors were silent, but every so often their wild calls rang out above the thunder. Primitive hairy men, huge and black on the skyline, flinging themselves across the ground in their primeval display of strength and power. And as each demonstrated his own majestic superiority, the women and children watched in silence. . . . For thirty minutes the wild display continued—and as I watched I could not help feeling the display was for my benefit—it was to me they were proving their strength and might. . . . Can you begin to imagine how I felt? The only human ever to have witnessed such a display, in all its primitive, fantastic wonder?"

Jane knew that she'd made a breakthrough when she witnessed the Rain Festival. It was a dramatic demonstration of the complexity of the lives of the wild chimps. She was making other breakthroughs as well. The most important was something less dramatic and more gradual—the chimpanzees' increasing comfort around their human observer. As early as November 1960, David Greybeard seemed to be completely at ease with Jane. On one occasion, Jane and David were both out walking and spotted each other. Jane sat down, and eventually David did the same, perfectly aware of the human watching him.

The chimpanzees continued to show new levels of comfort with Jane. On February 24, she reported that an adult male chimp ventured quite close to her camp to feed on the nuts of a nearby palm tree. Two days later, one of the staff members told Jane that a male chimp had been in the camp while she was away, again to eat nuts and other fruits. By mid-March, chimp sightings in camp were becoming common.

On March 30, Jane decided that she would wait for the chimps at camp rather than hike to look for them. At around one o'clock, she spotted two males near her tent. She snuck inside the tent to watch the apes from behind the cover of a tent flap. One of the apes was David Greybeard, and he seemed to stare back at Jane whenever she craned her neck to get a glimpse of him. On her twenty-seventh birthday, April 3, Jane was also visited by chimps in camp. She wrote to everyone at Bournemouth to say, "<u>What</u> a birthday present. . . . I had just penned the last word when I heard a noise, (I am <u>in</u> the tent, on bed, as it's cold) & saw a chimp hanging on the end of the frond of the palm tree outside. . . . He climbed up. I lay on my tummy & looked up at him. A second walked across to the frond. . . . This is the way to watch chimps. . . . WHAT a pity you're not here now Mum."

In need of additional funding, Louis had approached the National Geographic Society (NGS) in Washington, D.C., in February 1961. The NGS is a nonprofit organization devoted to promoting scientific and historical research and conservation. Louis argued that studying chimpanzee behavior was an important part of understanding human evolution. He also reported that his research assistant—Jane—had already spent time among the chimps and had made significant breakthroughs. His efforts won an additional $1,400 for Jane to continue on at Gombe. It was enough to support several more months of work.

When National Geographic put up the financial support for Jane's continued research, that funding came with the tacit agreement that the organization would be the first to publish photographs and a written account of Jane's work. Louis routinely embellished Jane's successes in his communications with National

Geographic, claiming that Jane came within fifteen to twenty feet of up to twenty-three chimpanzees while they were feeding. That was at least ten times closer than Jane usually got to the chimps. Louis's claims, however, reassured the National Geographic Society that Jane would be able to take good photographs of the animals. When asked why Jane hadn't produced any photographs yet, Louis let them believe she had not yet done so because he had not allowed it. He told National Geographic that Jane needed to let the chimps become comfortable with her by keeping completely still—even the slight movement of snapping a camera shutter would be enough to destroy the trust Jane was building with the chimpanzees. Louis argued that with additional time—and funds—Jane would be able to provide the photos that were desired.

National Geographic, however, was anxious for photos, and wanted one of their own photographers to take them. Jane was against a stranger entering her camp and capitalizing on her hard work. She wanted to take the photographs herself, or at least try to, before bringing in outside staff. In June 1961, Louis bought her a simple Retina Reflex camera to begin taking photographs in the field.

On August 14, Jane sent National Geographic one roll of film—the only roll she had shot. There were thirty-seven exposed frames on that roll, sixteen of which were too underexposed and ten of which were blurry. Of the rest, only one frame was potentially usable. National Geographic immediately declared Jane's first attempt at photography completely unsuitable.

Jane and Louis realized that someone other than Jane would have to be responsible for the photography, although neither conceded that a professional photographer was needed. Instead, they decided that Jane's sister Judy should come to Gombe to be the photographer for the chimp study.

Louis once again exaggerated the truth to National Geographic, claiming in a letter that Judy had "some experience of color photography," even though Judy's experience amounted to no more that Jane's. National Geographic balked at Louis's proposal and continued to insist that a professional photographer be used. The two sides were at an impasse, which Louis dealt with by ignoring the understood agreement with National

Geographic and selling the first publication rights for the story and pictures of Jane's chimpanzee work to a British newspaper, *Reveille*, for approximately $840.

In the meantime, Jane prepared for her sister's visit. She was sure that Judy would be a successful Gombe photographer, because she firmly believed that experience was not as necessary as "getting in the right place at the right time." Jane hoped that since she and Judy resembled each other, perhaps the chimps would think the sisters were both Jane if they both dressed in the same type of clothes.

Judy arrived in Gombe on September 23, 1961, with a new Nikon camera and assorted accessories, but Jane was not there to greet her. She had made another breakthrough—the day before, Jane had witnessed mating between the chimpanzees, and she was now in the field. Though she knew her sister was coming, she could not tear herself away. The following morning, Jane took Judy on her observation trip, and Judy was treated to the same rare sight.

Jane and Judy began to work on the chimp photography together, but their joint effort was as ineffective as Jane's solo attempt. They experienced repeated technical problems with the cameras. At first, Jane's Retina was out for repairs. Jane took over Judy's camera and was able to get fairly close to the chimps, but the lighting conditions and heavy cover from leaves and vines prevented her from getting any good photos. When the Retina came back after being repaired, Judy's camera was damaged by the heat and humidity of Gombe.

To Jane, the photographic failure was a personal failure. In a letter to Louis, she wrote, "I just can't help feeling miserable about everything." National Geographic decided that the photos were unsuitable for publication, and in January 1962, when Jane was back in England to begin her doctoral studies at Cambridge University, the Society notified her that it was no longer interested in publishing her story or her chimpanzee research.

Five

TWENTY-SEVEN-YEAR-OLD Jane set off for Cambridge on December 14, 1961, and found a home in a rooming house for young women at 1 Magrath Avenue. She registered at Newnham College, one of the three colleges at Cambridge University for women. Jane did not have an undergraduate degree, but by virtue of her work at Gombe and Louis's impressive powers of persuasion, Cambridge overlooked that. They counted her Gombe work as the basic research for her PhD, so she would only have to write and defend a thesis, a paper describing her research, to graduate.

To write the thesis, however, Jane needed to learn how to talk about her Gombe research in a scientific way. Her adviser at Cambridge was Professor Robert A. Hinde, who set about helping Jane transform her untrained observations into something more scientific. As such she would be trained in ethology, a scientific discipline with which she was completely unfamiliar. She wrote in a letter to Vanne, "The word was <u>ethology</u>—<u>not</u> ethnology, which (oddly enough) I know! I feel it may be a misprint for e<u>c</u>ology." Jane was wrong in thinking it was a misspelling; ethology is the study of animal behavior in a comparative way. Scientists think that animal behaviors are as distinctive to particular species as anatomy, and different species' behaviors can be compared just as their anatomies can.

Jane had used a technique called narrative observation to record her study of the Gombe chimpanzees. This meant that she wrote all of her comments like a story rather than use measurements or data points. This method allowed her the flexibility of keeping track of anything and everything, but it made it difficult to determine whether something was missed. Hinde helped her develop a more systematic approach. They designed checklists for chimpanzee behavior, including things such as grooming, feeding, or mating. Each checklist would be used for a certain period of time to mark what an individual chimp was doing in that time. Using the checklists, the observations would be standardized, allowing other researchers to participate in Jane's work. These checklists helped Jane begin to write up her results in a scientific format.

Part of ethology involves describing behaviors typical to a species, and Jane had no trouble doing this with chimps. She could easily talk about the six to seven hours a day a wild chimp spent feeding or the one to five minutes it took to build a nest. Jane had problems, however, with a different aspect of ethology. Traditionally, an ethologist focused on an entire species, looking for things common to all animals. But Jane was more interested in the individual chimps and the unique behaviors each might display. She gave her subjects names, as if they were as individual as people, which implied that they might have minds or feelings like people do. This caused friction between Jane and her professors. She later recalled, "When I began my study of wild chimpanzees in 1960 . . . it was not permissible, at least not in ethological circles, to talk about an animal's mind. Only humans had minds. . . . How naïve I was. . . . I did not realize that animals were not supposed to have personalities, or to think, or to feel emotions or pain. I had no idea that it would have been more appropriate—once I got to know him or her—to assign each of the chimpanzees a number rather than a name. I did not realize that it was unscientific to discuss behavior in terms of motivation or purpose." But Jane believed in her nontraditional methods and merely "ignored the admonitions of Science." She continued with her own scientific theories and did not change the chimps' names to numbers or change her methods going forward.

Despite her different scientific approach, by early 1962, Jane had made a lot of progress toward impressing the scientific world, though it was mostly through Louis's casual reports and the fact that he vouched for her. The previous August, while still at Gombe, she had been invited to a conference hosted by the Wenner-Gren Foundation in a castle in Austria. The conference was limited to only a select few scientists, so it was an honor for Jane to be included—especially since she didn't have a scientific degree. Jane was amused by the honor, writing to her family, "My future is so ridiculous. I just squat here, chimp-like, on my rocks, pulling out prickles & thorns, and laugh to think of this unknown 'Miss Goodall' who is said to be doing scientific research somewhere." She felt nervous about standing shoulder to shoulder with established scientists, so when she realized that the conference dates in July made it impossible for her to attend— she had already committed to being in Gombe for the entire summer doing field research—she may have been relieved.

Jane may have been uneasy about sharing her work, but the rest of the world was becoming increasingly interested. Louis wanted the NGS to reconsider supporting Jane's work and wrote an emphatic recommendation, saying, "The work she has done [is] completely outstanding and somehow I must raise the money to enable her to write it up quietly without having to try and earn enough to live on at the same time as writing it up."

Louis's appeal worked, and the NGS reversed its position. In January 1962, it sent an additional $1,124 to help support Jane during her first year at Cambridge.

The president of the Society, Melville Bell Grosvenor, explained that "the significance of these studies is extraordinary not to mention the excitement of Miss Goodall sitting there with these chimpanzees making friends with them and their unconcern when she is there. It would make a fabulous story for our magazine and we must make every effort to get it."

Soon, Jane received even more financial support from National Geographic. On March 22, the board of trustees voted to give Jane the Franklin L. Burr Prize for her contributions to science. This was not only a prestigious award, but worth $1,500 in cash. Still, the old problem of photographs reemerged when the Society renewed its support. This time around, it was clear that a professional photographer was needed. Jane still worried that an outsider would disrupt her carefully cultivated relationship with the chimpanzees, but it seemed that she had no other choice.

Jane did not have much of a chance to fret over the photographer, though. That same March, she was putting the last touches on her first scientific papers, "Feeding Behaviour of Wild Chimpanzees" and "Nest Building Behavior in the Free Ranging Chimpanzee."

With those completed, speaking at conferences was not something Jane could avoid for long, not if she wanted to be taken seriously by the scientific world. By April 11, a few days after she turned twenty-eight, Jane was on a train from Cambridge to London to attend and speak at a three-day symposium called "The Primates."

Jane's first two conference appearances as a speaker, in London and later at Yale University, were considered by many to be the first appearance of primatology as a modern science. Just as Louis had been excited about Jane's discovery of meat eating and tool use, these scientists shared that enthusiasm. The organizer of the symposium, John Napier, with whom Jane had briefly studied before setting out for Gombe, commented that "this woman has redefined humanity. I asked her to the conference because Louis said so. But it's quite extraordinary. This woman that nobody's ever heard of has appeared here on Louis's recommendation, and look at what she's been looking at."

With her lectures finished, Jane returned to Cambridge to finish the term and in July was headed back to Gombe. In the meantime, Louis had developed a solution to the photography problem. He convinced the National Geographic Society not only to underwrite the research at Gombe—a $5,000 commitment over one year—but also to pay Jane's expenses and the expenses of her mother. It was likely that the photographer chosen for the Gombe project would be a man—after all, there were far more male nature photographers than females ones—and Louis insisted that it would be improper for Jane to be alone in the jungle with him. Vanne would be Jane's official chaperone.

Louis was not about to let someone else, even in the National Geographic Society, decide what kind of photographer to send to participate in Jane's project. Since he had recruited Jane, and continued to act as her professional mentor, he felt extremely protective of her and her work. Therefore, Louis chose the Gombe photographer himself. He selected a young photographer who had done a good job with some of Louis's own projects, a Dutchman named Baron Hugo van Lawick.

Hugo held an aristocratic title, but his family did not have a great deal of wealth to go along with it, so Hugo had to earn a living. Since childhood, he had wanted to work with nature, and photography was a way to realize that dream. He had been working as a nature photographer for a few years before Louis chose him for Gombe. As much as his talents spoke for him, the fact that Hugo was already in Nairobi—and could get to Gombe in just a matter of days—also factored into Louis's selection process.

Jane returned to Gombe, which she now playfully called Chimpland, on July 8, 1962. For a few more weeks, Jane was on her own to conduct her research with only her African staff to help.

Jane soon discovered that the chimps had not forgotten her in the more than six months she had been gone and were still comfortable in her presence. David Greybeard and another male she called Goliath were enough at ease to come into her camp often in search of bananas.

By the time she returned to Gombe, Jane firmly believed that David was an important ape in the hierarchy of chimpanzees at Gombe. She felt that his calm and accepting attitude toward humans went a long way toward convincing the rest of the troop to trust her.

Jane described David and Goliath as tame, since they visited the camp regularly and even ventured into her tent. On the morning of August 17, in fact, Jane awoke to David Greybeard sitting next to her bed, eating a banana. Jane wasn't scared; in fact, she was amused, writing to her family, "He IS a devil! I shooed him off & closed my eyes. 5 mins later I heard a stealthy foot fall. When I shouted at him he spitefully gave the table a wham & knocked the thermos over!"

Later that same day, Jane had another breakthrough in building trust with the chimps. In the past, Jane had left bananas out for the chimps to steal, but that day, at noon, Jane held out a banana in her hand. David walked over to her and took the banana directly from her hand. It was the first time anyone had interacted with a wild chimpanzee in that way. Jane realized that she could leave bananas in the camp for the chimps to get them to venture closer. This would eliminate the difficulties of finding them in the field. The banana-feeding operation, which would grow over the years, was born.

Soon after the breakthrough with David Greybeard and the banana, in mid-August, Hugo arrived

Jane reaches for an infant chimp at Gombe.

in Gombe. Though Louis had insisted on a chaperone, Vanne would still not get there for a few more weeks, and Jane really didn't feel the need for supervision. She was looking forward to having Vanne in camp again, rather than feeling she needed her mother's protection from a stranger.

Jane wondered how she and Hugo would get along in the close quarters of camp. Her fears were allayed quickly since Hugo was as dedicated to his work as Jane was to hers. There were irritations—Hugo smoked heavily while Jane disliked the habit; Hugo was an atheist whereas Jane was spiritual—but the two settled into a comfortable coexistence. Jane wrote at the time to her friend Verdcourt, "We are a <u>very</u> happy family. Hugo is charming and we get on very well." In fact, the chimp that Jane had named Ugly was renamed Hugo in the photographer's honor.

Luckily for Hugo the human, he was able to capitalize on the trust Jane had built with the chimpanzees. Though he was a new individual, complete with large tripods, cameras, and lenses, the chimps seemed to tolerate him when he accompanied Jane around the forest. Hugo took photographs of Jane and the Gombe chimpanzees that finally pleased the National Geographic Society. In addition, he filmed Jane and the chimps for NGS-sponsored lectures that Jane might give in the future. By the end of December, the Society informed Jane that she should begin writing the article to accompany Hugo's photos.

Unknown to Jane, around the time that Louis had told her that he had found the right photographer for Gombe, he had also written to Vanne to say that he had found the right husband for Jane. And he seemed to be right. Sometime during their time together in the forest, Hugo and Jane developed feelings for each other. But Hugo left Gombe in early November for other assignments just after Vanne left for England, and Jane was scheduled to return to Cambridge in January for another term of graduate school. Their feelings were put on hold.

While Jane was away from Africa, her first priority was to complete the article for National Geographic. She did so by January 28, 1963, and by the time she received editorial suggestions for revisions, she was knee-deep both in her thesis and in a chapter for a book called *Primate Behavior: Field Studies of Monkeys and Apes.*

While at Cambridge, Jane had met a man named John King. They hit it off, and for a time she felt more strongly about him than she did about Hugo. John escorted her to the airport in London on March 25 for her flight to Nairobi. Jane spent the flight deep in thought, trying to figure out which relationship to pursue: John or Hugo. By the time she landed, Jane had settled on John. She worried that Hugo would take the news badly and that life at camp would become "quite ghastly."

Jane and Hugo returned to Gombe in April, and

they were immediately thrown back into their work. There was hardly time to decide on relationship issues. The chimps were still coming into camp for bananas; in fact, they were coming in greater numbers than before. Jane began to identify the family members of many of the chimps. She estimated that Flo's son Figan was six years old and her daughter Fifi was three. Olly was the mother of a daughter called Gilka and a seven- or eight-year-old male called Evered. Jane studied these family relationships carefully in the years ahead.

Jane and Hugo worked side by side for long hours, studying, photographing, and filming the apes. Jane wrote to her family that "our conversation is mostly— chimp—chimp—and more chimp. Hugo loves them as much as I do, and we have got a simply wonderful film as a result." In the course of working together, Jane changed her mind about which man, John or Hugo, she wanted to be with. She and Hugo grew very close.

Personally and professionally, it was an exciting time at Gombe. Jane and Hugo observed mating season and the behavior of several female chimps. They also witnessed the unusually close friendship of David Greybeard and Goliath. The two apes played together, groomed each other, protected each other, and supported each other. By that point David had grown comfortable enough with Jane to let her touch him, but when she did, Goliath responded with jealousy and aggression if he saw it.

In mid-July 1963, Vanne again returned to Gombe. She noticed that Jane and Hugo were "very happy with each other, and Jane is calm and happy. They discuss work and work and more work, and really and truly look very happy together. Jane is calm with Hugo and Hugo is good tempered all the time. . . . Hugo therefore has lasted longer than all the others in that his charm has survived a flit to England, a long separation and then a further stretch in Chimpland." By this point, Vanne was in no way a chaperone for Jane and Hugo, but National Geographic continued to pay for her expenses while she stayed at Gombe. Her responsibilities going forward had more to do with helping Jane in any way that she could.

Jane did not write about her feelings for Hugo at that time, but when Vanne left Gombe in mid-October, it is likely that Hugo moved into Jane's tent. Later, she wrote, "I had found in Hugo a companion with whom

I could share not only the joys and frustrations of my work, but also my love of the chimpanzees, of the forests and mountains, of life in the wilderness."

At the end of July, Jane received an advance copy of the August 1963 issue of *National Geographic*, which featured her article. It did a wonderful job of conveying both Jane's work and her personality to the world. After the article was published, Jane began to receive fan mail from people around the globe for the first time. People who had no scientific background wrote to Jane to tell her how her work inspired their own dreams of working with animals in the wild. One woman from Lima, Peru, asked if Jane needed an assistant, emphasizing that Jane would not be sorry if she was to give her a chance. Jane's former boss from her days at Schofield Productions, Stanley Schofield, asked if he could join her in Africa. The governor-general of Kenya wrote to tell Jane that he was so impressed by her article that he was having it bound in leather and giving it a place of honor on his bookshelf. The reception to Jane's story was bigger than anyone could have imagined.

At the same time, the *National Geographic* article brought fresh scrutiny of Jane and her work. One comment Jane frequently heard was that by providing bananas to the chimpanzees, she had altered their behavior from what it would normally be in the wild. This suggested Jane's work was not a true scientific study because she observed an artificial situation. But Jane's critics did not take into account that Gombe's trees provided fruit prolifically, so finding food was never a problem for the apes.

Jane, Hugo, and Vanne hardly had time to bask in the success of the article. The work continued, and on October 11, Jane had one of her most exciting experiences at Gombe. David Greybeard wandered into camp alone and then headed off to the Kasekela valley. With Hugo in tow, Jane followed David and soon found him sitting in the forest. She sat down next to him, and the two ate leaves together. Then Jane "found a palm nut . . . and felt sure that David would appreciate it. So I held it out on my outstretched palm. . . . [David] gave my offering a scornful glance and turned away. I held my hand a little nearer. . . . Suddenly, he turned towards me, reached out his hand to the nut, and, to my astonishment and delight, held my hand with his, keeping a firm warm pressure for about 10 seconds. He then withdrew his hand, glanced at the nut, and dropped it to the ground."

Jane was delighted. In her mind, David had shown her a gesture of reassurance and had tried to communicate with her as an equal. She no longer thought of the chimps as animals—to her they were conscious, emotional creatures as complex as human beings. She now felt responsible for their well-being and for their protection from the outside world.

Jane needed to return to Cambridge in 1964 because the university expected her to finish her thesis in consultation with her adviser in order to complete her degree. She hated to go away for a number of reasons. First, there was Hugo. Jane was in love, and for the first time, the relationship was surviving the test of time. Second, Jane worried about leaving Gombe without someone she trusted to run the camp. Hugo could not commit to it—he had his own career to consider and had to leave Gombe for other work.

Jane finally decided to abandon Cambridge altogether so she would not have to leave the chimps. She wanted to focus on a new goal—finding a way to set up and finance a permanent research station at Gombe. Louis agreed with the need for a research station but was alarmed by Jane's decision to abandon her degree. He understood more than Jane did that without the degree, it would be difficult for her to accomplish the things she wanted to do. Louis negotiated with Hinde at Cambridge on Jane's behalf to create a schedule that was more to her liking. They arranged for Jane to study at Cambridge for a shorter time, from January to March in 1964. After that she could return to Chimpland and remain there until the end of the year. In 1965, she would have to be in residence at the university for two terms and complete her thesis by the end of that academic year.

Louis also arranged for an English botanist named Kristopher Pirozynsky to take Jane's place in Gombe while she was at Cambridge. Pirozynsky would conduct his own botanical studies while ensuring that the Gombe camp continued to run smoothly—he would be observing the chimps, providing bananas, and keeping a record of anything momentous that might occur.

Pirozynsky arrived at Gombe in December 1963 and spent a few days with Jane, familiarizing himself with the camp. Jane was satisfied that Pirozynsky would take good care of Chimpland and was at ease when she left for Nairobi with Hugo on December 15. From there, Jane headed back to Cambridge. Hugo remained in Nairobi until it was time for him to go on another photo safari.

On December 26, while Jane was home at Bournemouth, she received a telegram from Hugo: WILL YOU MARRY ME LOVE HUGO. Jane telegrammed immediately in reply to say yes, though the prospective groom had to wait to hear her answer. He had left on safari and could not call in to Nairobi to read her reply for five days. The wedding was set for March 28, 1964, a few days before the bride's thirtieth birthday.

While planning the wedding, Jane worked on her first big public lecture, scheduled for February 28 at the 3,500-seat Constitution Hall in Washington, D.C., something that she "dreaded most terribly, but managed to survive, acquiring some experience while at the same time sharing some of [her] knowledge." She also had a more scientifically advanced lecture to the National Academy of Sciences scheduled for March 2. And she was still working on her thesis at Cambridge.

It was a hectic time, and Jane confessed to friends that she was worn out. When the exhaustion gave way to unusual fatigue, Jane had herself examined at the Tropical Diseases Hospital in London. She worried that she might have a parasitic disease. Luckily, she did not, and the bride was well enough to attend her own wedding.

The ceremony was held at Chelsea Old Church in London, where Jane had been christened. The bride wore a white dress and the bridesmaids wore yellow. The reception hall was decorated with lilies, daffodils, and large color photographs of Jane's absent chimpanzee friends—David, Goliath, Flo, and Fifi. A clay model of David Greybeard served as the cake topper. Louis sent a tape-recorded congratulatory speech along with his daughter and granddaughter to convey their good wishes. And a telegram was read at the reception that announced that Jane had received her second Franklin L. Burr Prize, this time for $2,000, from the National Geographic Society. Jane had a lot to celebrate, and her future never seemed so bright.

Six

JANE AND HUGO planned to honeymoon for four days in Holland. The trip was cut short, though, by news from Gombe—Flo had had a baby. Jane had observed Flo during mating season and suspected that she might have gotten pregnant the previous year. When Pirozynsky telegrammed with the news of the baby, Jane's suspicions were confirmed.

Jane and Hugo hurried back to Africa, arriving at camp on April 14, 1964. Jane was anxious to meet Flo's baby, soon called Flint. She was disappointed that she had not been present for the birth. Pirozynsky reported that for the first few weeks, Flint hardly moved, and it was only two days before Jane's arrival that the baby had begun to look around. Jane found Flint to be "simply the most adorable little object you ever saw."

Before her wedding, Jane had written to Louis to say that she was looking for an assistant. The woman from Peru who had written in response to the *National Geographic* article, Edna Koning, had impressed Jane with her impassioned plea and her perfect typing. Koning had a psychology degree from Reed College in the United States, and Jane decided to give her a chance. When Koning arrived at Gombe, Jane entrusted the time-consuming task of transcribing her recorded field notes to her.

The most important problem that Jane and Hugo had to tackle was adjusting the banana-feeding procedures in the camp. When they had been at Gombe before their wedding, bananas were left haphazardly in baskets around camp for the chimps. Over time this caused a number of problems, including fighting when chimps hoarded bananas. Also, the chimps often walked right into the human residences looking for bananas. The apes were happy to raid anything in search of the fruit, and possessions were being destroyed. Pirozynsky had observed the chimps chewing on clothing and bedding, until Goliath discovered canvas. Soon, groups of chimps came to camp to chew on canvas—in the form of tents, camp chairs, and beds.

Jane watches Hugo adjust a camera while a baboon looks on, Gombe, 1974.

The canvas chewing only lasted, though, until the chimps discovered wood. Jane and Hugo came back to Gombe to discover that a chair leg and the back of a cupboard had been destroyed by visiting apes.

The fishermen began to be victimized by the chimps' raids as well. They, of course, were unhappy to have chimpanzees destroy their huts and belongings, and Jane and Hugo worried that violence might break out between the humans and the chimps. They had to find a new way to leave bananas for the chimpanzees immediately.

First, they decided to move the banana-feeding operation away from the camp and the fishermen's huts. Hugo and Jane found a new spot about a half mile away and they named it Ridge Camp, in contrast to the old campsite, now called Lake Camp. Since they had realized even before Jane had left for school that the banana feedings could cause problems, Hugo, while he was in Nairobi, had designed and ordered ten steel boxes that could be opened remotely for dispersing the bananas.

When they returned to Gombe, though, the boxes had not yet arrived. Instead, Hassan used sheets of corrugated iron to build a large storage area for bananas at Ridge Camp. Early one morning, Jane waited at the new provisioning area, but the chimps did not know to go there for their bananas. Hugo, still at Lake Camp, contacted Jane on the walkie-talkie at nine o'clock to say that a number of chimps were waiting there. He realized that he had to lead them to the new location.

With Jane listening on the walkie-talkie, Hugo grabbed one of the corrugated banana boxes and waved it at David Greybeard. When he had gotten the chimps' attention, Hugo began sprinting up to Ridge Camp. Jane could hardly understand his breathless, garbled pleas—but eventually she realized that he wanted her to toss bananas along the path between the camps. She wrote, "I rushed about with armfuls of fruit and had just finished my task when Hugo appeared, running along with a box under one arm and a single banana in his other hand. He hurled the one fruit along the path and collapsed beside me, gasping for breath, as the group of chimps which had been following him suddenly saw the bananas all over the path. With piercing shrieks of excitement they hugged and kissed and patted one another as they fell on the unexpected feast."

A few days after this, the other chimps also learned about Ridge Camp by following individuals that had found the new provisioning area. Since the new location was deeper in the forest, more chimpanzees felt comfortable visiting the humans there. Jane identified several more chimps because of it. She began to notice so many new, previously undocumented behaviors that she could barely keep track of them all. Jane and Hugo discovered many more types of chimpanzee food, such as weaver ants and caterpillars. Jane saw the chimps catch termites in midair as they swarmed, snatching them with their hands. She and Hugo were inspired by the large quantities of weaver ants that the chimps ate and decided to try them. Jane wrote that the ants "have a most exotic flavour, and [she and Hugo were] planning ways of marketing them as tropical delicacies!"

The banana-box issue was not completely resolved, though. The camp staff continued to experiment with other homemade solutions until the custom-ordered steel banana boxes finally arrived on August 10. The steel boxes, along with some concrete boxes with steel lids, were set up at Ridge Camp. The lids of both types could be controlled remotely by wires and levers, and were much more successful in controlling the amount of bananas provided to the chimps at any time.

Ridge Camp not only drew the chimpanzees away from the beach and the fishermen, but it also provided

Jane and Hugo some newlywed privacy. They set up their own living quarters there and luxuriated in their "own special little tent." Even though they were out in the wilderness, they created some normal domesticity in their lives. They cooked breakfast and ate lunch together with sunbirds feeding on nectar nearby. They had two canvas baths that they set up side by side so that they could scrub each other's backs when they bathed. In the evenings, while bushbucks ambled across the grass, they washed in a nearby stream before the staff brought up their dinners.

Jane continued making new discoveries and felt that her observations of the newborn chimps, especially Flo's baby Flint, were the most important. No one had ever watched the development of a chimpanzee in the wild from such an early age. Jane documented Flint's first steps and first teeth, and observed closely how Flo raised him. Flo was indulgent and playful, often ticking and cuddling the baby. Jane even noticed that Flint's sister, Fifi, seemed to be getting some training for motherhood by helping Flo take care of her brother. Fifi sometimes groomed Flint, carried him, or played with him.

Later, in her autobiography *My Life with the Chimpanzees*, Jane admitted that "because chimpanzees are so like humans, and because each has his or her own unique character, there have been some individuals that I have not liked very much, some that were just okay, and some that I have liked very much indeed." Flo was one of the chimps that Jane loved, and with the birth of Flint, Flo and her family became central to Jane's research study.

In June 1964, a National Geographic staff member named Joanne Hess arrived at Gombe to oversee filming for a planned television documentary about Jane and the chimpanzees. Jane was annoyed at the visit, since Hess wanted to script and film some human-interest aspects of the documentary. This took time away from Jane's research, but she was forced to pose and reenact on cue for three weeks.

Jane had good reason to keep National Geographic happy, though, since that year Jane and Hugo, with the help of Louis, had finally secured funding for the permanent research facility at Gombe. The National Geographic Society awarded Jane a grant for $13,428.20—$9,920.40 for the chimp study during

1965 and $3,508.40 for prefabricated huts to use for the research center.

In mid-February 1965, the new buildings were put together at a new site a half mile from Ridge Camp. The larger building had one main workroom and two smaller sleeping quarters and was nicknamed Pan Palace, after part of the scientific name of chimpanzees, *Pan troglodytes*. The smaller building, a single room for Jane and Hugo, was called Lawick Lodge. By the beginning of March, thirty remote-operated banana boxes had been set up at the research center. Jane gave the newly built area an official name: the Gombe Stream Research Centre.

With the research station up and running, Jane and Hugo prepared to leave Gombe temporarily. Only Koning, who had been promoted to perform research duties, and Jane's new assistant Sonia Ivey, as well as the African staff, would remain at Gombe. Koning and Ivey took responsibility for the chimpanzee observations. After a short holiday at the Masai Mara Game Reserve, Jane and Hugo went to Dar es Salaam, where Jane gave a lecture for President Julius Nyerere. By April 11, they were back in Nairobi, preparing for a brief separation. Hugo headed off on assignment for National Geographic to take photographs for a book about East African animals. Jane, who had just turned thirty-one, was on her way back to Cambridge for her studies for the rest of the year.

Jane felt sad about leaving Gombe, especially since she had recently identified another female chimp, Madame Bee, that had begun to come to the banana-provisioning area frequently with her daughter Little Bee and newborn Honey Bee. Jane wrote at the time, "How sad that we shall miss the story of Little Bee and Honey Bee. But how <u>lucky</u> to have someone to record it all and know that the facts will not be lost for ever."

Upon Jane's return to Cambridge, she worked tirelessly on her thesis. In addition, she was working on more articles about the chimp research. She also had a number of presentations to write for scientific conferences around the world. Jane was so busy that she worked herself to exhaustion. A friend reported that she barely ate more than the occasional apple with coffee. By the end of July, her health got so bad that she was hospitalized for anemia and a minor infection.

Jane returned home to Bournemouth for a few days to recuperate before heading off to a conference in Austria.

In the meantime, Louis decided to intercede on Jane's behalf. He contacted Jane's adviser, Hinde, and reminded him that Jane had already typed more than eight thousand pages of scientifically important journal notes. Since a thesis was supposed to be a complete written report of a PhD student's research, Louis felt those journal notes should be considered Jane's thesis. He explained that with Hinde's permission, she could add an introduction and conclusion to those notes and hand them in to fulfill the requirements for her degree. Hinde agreed.

While Louis negotiated, Hugo met up with Jane in England, and they went to the conference in Austria together. Afterward they planned to take a short holiday at a chalet nearby. While Jane conferred with colleagues, obviously a star, Hugo felt awkward and isolated. Jane felt he was jealous of her, after dinner on the second night, she found him alone in their room, lying on the bed, angrily smoking a cigarette. When he saw Jane, they argued bitterly, and Jane was so hurt that she cried for hours. For the first time, Jane worried that her marriage would not last.

After the symposium, when Jane was no longer the center of attention, Hugo's mood improved, and by October 11, they were both back in England briefly before Hugo left, first for National Geographic headquarters in Washington, D.C., then for another Geographic-funded photo safari in Nairobi. Jane went back to Cambridge to take up her thesis work again.

On December 16, Jane finished her thesis, just in time to enjoy the cover of the new issue of *National Geographic*, which featured a picture of her alongside Flo, Fifi, Flint, and many other chimps. She was becoming quite a celebrity, and she became even more famous on December 22 when CBS broadcast the television special *Miss Goodall and the Wild Chimpanzees*. When the show aired, the real Jane was back in Nairobi, not glued to the television set but chatting comfortably with her husband.

New criticisms emerged with her fame. Some people suggested that Jane was popular because she was pretty and looked good in shorts. Older criticisms that Jane's work wasn't true scientific study also resurfaced. Leonard Carmichael, the chairman of the Committee for Research and Exploration at the National Geographic Society, defended Jane, saying she was "the most qualified person in the world today to speak on the subject of chimpanzee behavior." This endorsement helped silence at least some of her critics.

Jane defended her thesis on February 9 and earned the right to call herself Dr. van Lawick-Goodall. The newly minted doctor flew to the United States on February 13 for a new set of lectures at Constitution Hall, the first of which gathered a huge crowd of 3,500. A reporter covering the first event noticed that Jane looked a great deal like a deer in headlights, but her presentations were well received. Hugo and Vanne were in the audience for Jane's lectures, as guests of National Geographic, and Hugo stayed on with her through some of her next stops.

Jane followed these successful lectures with a tour all over the United States. Her schedule also included a stop at National Geographic headquarters in Washington, D.C., to secure more funding for Gombe. The budget meeting was a new frontier for her. Before that, Louis had taken care of most of the funding requests.

But now that Jane had received her PhD, she was a serious scientist in her own right, and she would need to begin the lifelong task of lecturing about and raising money for the research on the chimps.

In May 1966, Jane and Hugo were finally back in Gombe, where the faces had changed once again. Koning and Ivey were gone for good, and in their place was an older woman named Sally Avery, who moved into Pan Palace with a researcher named Caroline Coleman. John MacKinnon, who had arrived months earlier to study Gombe's insects, lived a short distance away from Ridge Camp, and Hugo's half brother, Michael, was visiting. They, along with the African staff, welcomed Jane and Hugo back.

Jane settled back into her routine of observing the apes. Soon after, some of the younger chimps—Fifi, Figan, and Evered—figured out how to remove the pins from the lever handles that kept the concrete banana boxes shut. The older apes never seemed to learn the trick and relied on the youngsters to do the dirty work. But the trio wasn't always in the mood to share. Sometimes they would wait until the older chimps left the camp before pressing the lever and opening a banana box. The result was that the chimps spent very long amounts of time in camp or in the surrounding valley.

Jane wrote that "we were horrified at the change we saw in the chimps' behaviour. Not only was there a great deal more fighting than ever before, but many of the chimps were hanging around in camp for hours and hours every day. This was almost entirely due to Fifi and Figan and . . . Evered." Jane had Hassan replace the pins with screws, thinking that the chimps would find them more difficult to remove. But within a few months, the trio figured out how to unscrew those as well. Jane was impressed and amused by their antics, but she realized that the camp needed a new feeding system.

Jane upgraded to steel boxes with battery-operated locks to keep the resourceful chimps from stealing bananas. The locks could be opened by pressing buttons on the control panels located within Lawick Lodge. Because the locks were electronic, it was more difficult to disassemble them, and since the chimps did not see the buttons being pressed, they did not learn what the humans were doing. Jane gleefully wrote that the new system "should really fox cunning little devils like Fifi!!"

With the banana-box issue temporarily resolved, Jane became very busy with writing a book about her life at Gombe for National Geographic. By July, she sent the final chapters to Vanne to get her opinion before she submitted the manuscript to her editors. The book, *My Friends The Wild Chimpanzees*, was published in 1967.

Jane also began to seriously consider writing her own book, independent of National Geographic and its interests. She had been approached by publishers, and offered significant amounts of money, but Jane had signed a literary release years before with the NGS that meant she could only publish with the Society's approval. As long as she depended on its funds, the NGS had the right to block other books. Still, Jane dreamed about the book she would someday write and had even decided to title it *In the Shadow of Man*. The book itself, though, would have to wait.

That summer, Jane and Hugo went to the Serengeti together in their Volkswagen bus. The goal was for Hugo to photograph the local wildlife, but when they arrived, they found that a fire had spread through the plain, leaving few animals in sight. Jane and Hugo came upon a male ostrich guarding a nest of five eggs, and marveled that the bird and his nest survived the fire. They also saw a large bird circling overhead. They followed the bird and discovered a second ostrich nest full of eggs, surrounded by different types of vultures. Two of the birds were Egyptian vultures, a species much smaller than the other vultures gathered there. While the larger birds squabbled over eggs that were already broken, the Egyptian vultures took stones in their beaks, reared up high, and then threw the stones down on the unbroken egg. The hard eggshells broke, and the Egyptian vultures were able to feast.

This event was a huge discovery. Until then only five animals were known to use tools: California sea otters, which cracked shellfish on stones on their chests while swimming on their backs; Galápagos woodpecker finches, which used twigs or cactus spines to search for grubs; sand wasps, which used small stones as hammers; marine crabs, which held stinging sea anemones as shields; and chimpanzees, as Jane had observed.

Now she could document the use of a tool by a brand-new animal. Jane wrote at the time that the discovery was "so exciting we can hardly believe it."

On August 26, Jane telegrammed news of the vultures and their tools to the president of the National Geographic Society, Melville Bell Grosvenor. Soon after, Jane and Hugo wrote several articles about their discovery, including one for *National Geographic* that appeared in the May 1968 issue. The publicity from this latest observation meant that Dr. Jane van Lawick-Goodall became even more admired by scientists and the general public alike.

In a second telegram on the same day, Jane reported that the chimp called Olly had had another baby, named Grosvenor in honor of the president himself. But Jane's joy in recording Grosvenor's birth turned almost immediately to sorrow. From the beginning, Jane noticed that Grosvenor screamed as if he was in pain any time Olly moved when he was trying to rest. Soon, he appeared to be paralyzed from the neck down. Later that day, Jane followed Olly as she carried her baby up to a tree to nurse him. When Olly came down from the tree, Grosvenor was unusually quiet and still. Jane suspected that the baby had died.

The following day, Olly and her daughter Gilka brought Grosvenor's dead body to the provisioning area. Jane wrote, "It was unutterably horrible. And the stench was enough to make one sick." Jane mourned with Olly over her loss, and worried about the other chimps.

In November, when Gilka came to camp, Jane noticed that Gilka's wrist was paralyzed. Soon afterward, Flo's oldest son, Faben, and another chimp, Madame Bee, were each seen with their arms paralyzed. And other apes had similar problems—Jane saw many of them dragging paralyzed feet or hands. Olly began to have trouble walking on one foot, and David Greybeard was not able to put any weight on one leg. Eventually, Jane and Hugo realized that polio was afflicting the Gombe chimps.

Polio is an infectious disease that often causes paralysis in humans and in chimpanzees. The virus that causes polio can be spread orally, and polio cases had been reported among the residents of two villages between Gombe and Kigoma. It was likely that the chimps had picked up the virus by eating discarded food from the villages.

Jane and Hugo radioed Louis to arrange for

polio vaccines to be delivered for the humans working near the chimps. As soon as all the people in Gombe were vaccinated, Jane and Hugo began to treat the chimpanzees as well. Doses of vaccine were inserted into bananas, and Jane created a chart to track which chimps ate medicated bananas and what doses they got. It was tricky to dispense the vaccine—too little and the chimp could still contract the disease, too much and the chimp was likely to develop polio from the vaccine. Jane wrote, "The whole affair has been like living in a nightmare." She felt overwhelmed and despondent, and couldn't even summon the energy to write home.

Jane and Hugo left for Nairobi on December 19. The polio epidemic seemed to be under control, but it was not a particularly joyful holiday season. Jane wrote, "Bells and trees & plum puddings all seemed so out of place." When the couple returned to Gombe in January 1967, they learned that four chimps were dead, five suffered from partial paralysis, and the rest had been successfully vaccinated.

The polio epidemic had been exhausting for Jane, especially since, by that time, she was seven months pregnant. She and Hugo were trying to keep the pregnancy a surprise for friends and family, though it became increasingly difficult as her stomach got bigger and bigger. On her trip to Nairobi at the end of December, there was no way to hide the news from Louis; he, in turn, likely told Vanne. Jane's sister Judy found out when a coworker at the British Museum of Natural History asked her how she felt about becoming an aunt.

Jane had spent years studying the relationships between chimpanzee mothers and their infants, and now she was looking forward to studying her own infant. She decided that, like chimpanzee mothers, she wanted close and extended contact with her baby. At the time, newborn babies were normally kept separate from mothers to give both an opportunity to recover from the birth. Jane had seen that the birthing process did not affect a chimp's ability to care for a newborn and believed that the same would be true for her. So she and Hugo found a small Catholic hospital in Nairobi that allowed mothers to keep their babies close from birth.

Even though Jane was pregnant, her life continued at the same busy pace. She spent much of her time inside the Ngorongoro Crater, studying vultures with Hugo, following up on their earlier observations. They watched older Egyptian vultures pick up small stones with their beaks and throw them against ostrich eggs, while younger vultures merely pecked at the shells. From this, Jane surmised that vultures learned to use stones as tools by watching older birds and imitating them.

One night in the crater, Hugo and Jane encountered a very different kind of animal—a lion on the prowl. They were sitting in their office tent with one side flipped up; it was almost dark, and the two were working by the light of a very bright gas lantern. Their Land Rover was parked close to the tent, in case of emergency, as was always the case when they were in the wild.

The two staff members accompanying the van Lawicks spotted the lion, but Jane and Hugo had not yet seen it. One of them cried out to warn Hugo and even pointed a flashlight at the lion. But Hugo could not understand what was being said. Instead of taking cover, Hugo walked out into the open to see what was going on. He was faced with the lion about twenty yards away, and creeping closer. He immediately rushed back to the tent to usher the very pregnant Jane toward the Land Rover.

But a second lion was blocking their way to the Land Rover, so Jane and Hugo returned to the tent and lit torches, hoping the lions would avoid the bright fire. The staff, hiding in the kitchen tent, saw that a lion was blocking the path to the vehicle. They started blasting the radio and banging on pots and pans to distract the animal. It worked, but when Hugo opened the flap of the office tent again, he heard the sneeze of a third lion right next to the Land Rover.

Hugo and Jane began to hear the sounds of canvas ripping and worried that the staff was being attacked. Desperate, they lit wads of paper to throw at the lions. But then they heard the car doors slamming—the two staff members had somehow made it safely to the Land Rover.

Three lions began investigating the kitchen tent, and Jane and Hugo saw their opportunity to race to the Land Rover. Safely inside, they tried to chase the lions away by driving the vehicle straight at them. The big cats, however, thought the car was being playful.

For a while, they merely leaped and pounced in response. Finally, Hugo and Jane managed to drive the lions away with the Land Rover—right after the kitchen tent caught fire from their earlier attempts to get rid of their unwanted guests. They used fire extinguishers to put out the fire, and then Hugo and Jane immediately headed toward a little log cabin nearby, intent on spending the rest of the trip protected by solid walls.

When they arrived, however, they saw that a large, black-maned male lion stood on the veranda while his lioness feasted on a freshly killed antelope behind the cabin. Jane and Hugo had to wait, helpless, until the male left, and then they stealthily snuck into the cabin. Jane and Hugo bolted themselves inside while the African staff did the same inside the nearby kitchen cabin. When the tension of the evening finally faded and the van Lawicks had caught their breath, they joked that they would name their child Simba, Swahili for "lion," in honor of the experience.

Seven

BY THE END of February 1967, Jane and Hugo were back in Nairobi, awaiting the birth of their child. They lived in the Devon Hotel until they found a stone house with a tile roof in Limuru, about eighteen miles outside of town. The house had a spectacular view, lovely gardens, and, as the seller pointed out to Hugo, a beautiful back veranda, a perfect spot for a wife to sit and sew. Of course, Jane was not interested in traditional feminine pastimes such as sewing, but the van Lawicks bought the house anyway.

Jane went into labor around two o'clock in the morning on March 4, and the baby boy was born at 9:45 A.M. A night nurse, convinced that the process would take much longer, sent Hugo back to bed, so he missed the birth completely.

Jane had been excited that the hospital would let her keep her baby close from birth, but in the end, the staff did not allow her to keep the baby in her room. This was a great disappointment to Jane. She wrote: "Hugo & I have given up. . . . As I hope to be out in 2 more days, or 3 perhaps, we have resigned ourselves to all the possible repressions & fixations and complexes etc, etc which may develop in his personality as a consequence." From her work with the chimpanzees, Jane knew that early contact between mother and child was important. She wanted to repeat that with her son but was given no choice in the matter.

Traditionally, in the van Lawick family, first sons were named Hugo, but Jane also wanted to honor her uncle Eric and Louis Leakey. So the couple named the baby Hugo Eric Louis van Lawick, despite the regrettable sequence of initials.

There was never any question about Jane giving up her Gombe research—she would not do that. But she did understand that a newborn couldn't be toted to the jungle from the day he was born. The new family went back to the Devon Hotel until April 2, when the Limuru house was ready. Jane kept busy with her research, interviewing a new secretary and hosting a new research assistant, Patrick McGinnis. The day after moving the family into the Limuru house, Big Hugo, as he was now called, flew back to Gombe to settle McGinnis and to take care of the research center's administrative duties. A few days later, Jane and Little Hugo flew to England to the Birches, where Little Hugo met his grandmother, great-grandmother, aunt, and other relations. On May 5, Little Hugo was christened in the same church where his parents had been married.

Jane returned to Nairobi with baby in tow in June 1967, heading to the house in Limuru to find it full of flowers from Hugo. Life with a newborn was mostly as she expected—there were days when Little Hugo cried and cried for no reason, and times when he slept peacefully and played happily.

At the end of June, Jane and Little Hugo went to Gombe. A steel cage was already set up inside Lawick Lodge to protect the baby through the night from any wild visitors to camp. Jane knew that chimpanzees sometimes fed on baby baboons, and she was not about to test whether human babies would be just as tempting. The cage was painted bright blue, and Jane hung birds and stars from its ceiling. It was large enough to hold a safari cot, the baby carriage, and a chair, as well as Little Hugo and his mother. Later, some people would criticize Jane's decision to raise her son at Gombe, and the cage in particular was cited as troubling. But Jane ignored any disapproval; she never intended to be separated from her child.

Jane was finding it tiring to say Big Hugo and Little Hugo to distinguish between husband and son. Her son was extremely messy, and so to avoid confusion with his father, she nicknamed him Grublin, a name that would often be shortened merely to Grub.

In Jane's opinion, Grub had a "most extraordinary life." He spent almost all of his early life by Jane's side, whether she was in England, Limuru, or the forests of Gombe. Jane and Hugo took special precautions to keep Grub safe from their wild neighbors at Gombe. In addition to the cage, when Grub learned to walk, they built and moved into a new house on the beach where the chimps did not often wander. The house even had a caged-in veranda on which Grub could play.

After Grub's birth, Jane went into the field less frequently and focused on the best way to be a mother. She wrote, "I had to choose between various sources of advice. There was my own mother, there was Dr. Spock [a noted child-care expert]—and there was Flo." And just as Jane had looked to chimpanzee mothers as examples when she considered the birth of her child, the chimpanzee mothers, especially Flo, were influential in the way Jane raised Grub. Jane observed that chimp mothers such as Flo that were affectionate and tolerant raised babies that had good adult relationships and were successful community members. But there was a chimp named Passion that was far more harsh and less caring in her child rearing. Passion's babies were tense and ill at ease as adults. Jane kept those examples in mind with Grub, and wrote, "There is no doubt that my observation of the chimpanzees helped me to be a better mother."

Reducing her time in the field also allowed Jane to better perform administrative duties for Gombe, including writing reports and articles and requesting funding. There were soon new researchers at camp, including chimp observers Patricia Moehlman, Geza Teleki, and Ruth Davis, and baboon observers Tim and Bonnie Ransom, all of whom had to be supervised. Additionally, many visitors came to Gombe, including Tanzania's minister of agriculture Derek Bryceson. Life was full and hectic.

The next few years held a number of challenges for Jane and Hugo. Early in 1968, a deadly flu epidemic swept through the animals at Gombe. Jane and Hugo were not there at the time, but they kept in touch with Gombe twice a week by radiotelephone. They soon heard that David Greybeard was among the victims of the epidemic, which devastated Jane. She wrote, "I still cannot believe [he] has gone, and hardly like to write of it."

There were more chimpanzee losses as well. Several babies died in infancy. Jane's old friend Flo gave birth to a new dau_ater, Flame, in July 1968, but sadly, Flame died the following February. Jane suspected that she held on as long as she could but eventually had become a victim of the flu.

To add to the problems, the banana-feeding system needed another overhaul. Around three dozen chimps

Evered, Faben, Figan, and Hugo sit in a line next to a baby chimp, 1974.

routinely waited at camp for bananas, even though the fruit was only offered on seven out of any fourteen days. Additionally, a few dozen baboons, which also liked free fruit, began to linger in camp. The human observers were often caught in the middle when fights broke out between the chimps and baboons. The baboons feared larger humans such as Teleki, who had a good aim with stones, but were not intimidated by slender Davis. One day, a baboon attacked Davis. Luckily, she only had a scratch on the elbow, but Jane was concerned enough to order a reduction in the number of scheduled feedings.

The van Lawicks had other difficulties not directly related to the research. They began to have financial problems. For most of their personal needs, the family was dependent on Hugo's advance payment for his book *Innocent Killers*, which he started planning back in mid-1967. But that money was going fast, and the manuscript was progressing very slowly. Christmas 1968 was grim—the only decorations on their sparse, silvery foil tree were ones from their families.

To get them through the rough patch, Jane decided to help Hugo write his book. Soon she was shouldering much of the responsibility for the manuscript, even getting permission from the publisher to entirely write one of the chapters herself. The book became a joint effort by husband and wife. Jane also created a children's book with Hugo's photographs of Grub, and the money from that project helped ease the family's financial strain, though it kept her from working on her own projects, including her long-planned book.

But by far the worst challenge for Jane came on July 13, 1969, when Jane's student Ruth Davis had a tragic accident. Davis had been following one of the chimps, Mike, and did not return to camp that night. A search began by everyone at the research center and even some of the fishermen, but for six days, no one knew where she was. Finally, on July 19, her body was found at the bottom of a waterfall in Kahama valley, far to the south of the camp.

Jane was crushed by Davis's death. She wrote of feeling responsible because Davis would never have been at Gombe if not for Jane's chimp research. The tragedy led to a policy change at the research center: No student would be allowed to go into the field without being accompanied by a local Tanzanian staff member. As Jane wrote, "If only [Davis] had not been on her own—a companion could have at least returned to tell us where she was. And so Hilali Matama, Eslom Mpongo, Hamisi Mkono, Yahaya Alamasi, and many others joined our field staff."

That policy was in full force by 1970, when Jane and her researchers discovered that the chimps of Gombe were also making changes. In nature, an alpha male is a powerful figure, the one in society that runs the show. The chimp named Mike had been the top-ranking male, and the rest of the chimps showed him respect and deference. But Mike was getting old; his hair had thinned and his teeth had ground down. Flo's son Figan began to ignore Mike and encouraged Evered to do so as well. Figan also convinced his brother Faben to turn against Mike, and Faben, in turn, encouraged his friend Humphrey to do the same. Humphrey was a big and aggressive bully, and eventually, with Faben's help, he challenged Mike and won, and became the alpha male.

But Jane expected that one day Humphrey would be replaced as alpha male, and Figan and Evered would compete for the top-ranking spot. "Hugo and I suspect that eventually Figan will become the top-ranking male. . . . For Figan is not only more intelligent than Evered—he also has the backing of a large family. The proximity of Faben will probably always give him . . . confidence." And true enough, in July 1970, Figan and Faben got into a major fight with Evered. Together, the brothers seriously injured Evered, resulting in Figan moving up in the hierarchy of apes. Figan soon decided it was his opportunity to get rid of Humphrey.

On February 8, 1973, Jane wrote to her family,

"Figan is still challenging Humphrey, backed by Faben." Humphrey was older and stronger, but again Figan relied on his brains rather than his brawn for success. While Humphrey could easily overpower Figan alone, Figan only challenged Humphrey when Faben was around. After several repeated attacks, Humphrey never tried to dominate Figan again. Figan had won the rank of alpha male.

It took years for Jane to fully witness and document the power struggles in the chimp community, but in 1970, she was a participant in a different battle with a different type of alpha male. The top-ranking men at the National Geographic Society had decided that they were not interested in fully funding the research at Gombe anymore. They cut their annual grant from $40,000 to $25,000. They believed that the Society had made Jane famous, and now Jane should secure funding elsewhere. They informed Jane that though they were reducing her funds, they expected that the research budget would stay the same. She should consider the cuts as coming from her and Hugo's salaries. In response, Jane informed the Society that without a salary, she and Hugo could not afford to spend their time exclusively at Gombe.

The up side of the funding cut—which meant National Geographic had less influence at Gombe— was that Jane could finally pursue other opportunities for supporting and developing Gombe. One came through Jane's friendship with Dr. David A. Hamburg, the chairman of Stanford University's Department of Psychiatry. Hamburg had visited Gombe in the summer of 1968, and Jane had discussed her financial problems with him then. He had suggested that he might be able to help by sending Jane researchers, and possibly graduate students, who would qualify for additional grant money that could be added to the Gombe pool of resources. Also, Hamburg had said that he would try to get money from the National Institute of Child Health & Human Development to fund the production of scientific films on chimp development.

Jane and Hamburg both wanted to create a formal affiliation between Stanford and Gombe, and by late 1970, this was almost finalized. Hamburg also provided an additional affiliation with the University of Dar es Salaam. And finally, Hamburg helped Jane secure annual funding for Gombe from the William T. Grant Foundation, the same organization that funded Hamburg's Stanford Outdoor Primate Facility. Jane, of course, preferred to think of that facility as Gombe West.

Because of these new affiliations, Jane started giving lectures at the University of Dar es Salaam in Tanzania and traveled to California twice a year to teach and participate in the research at Stanford. But her permanent base was still Gombe.

Jane was very grateful to Hamburg and the Grant Foundation for essentially saving Gombe. With the annual-funding issue dealt with, she was finally able to turn her attention to her long-planned book. In April 1970, Jane returned to England with three-year-old Grub so that her son could become acquainted with the family and she could begin work on *In the Shadow of Man*. Her publisher had paid her an impressive $100,000 for the book, but that money did not change Jane's life in any meaningful way. The bulk of it was placed in an irrevocable trust for Grub, meaning that

Jane legally gave the money to Grub and she could not change her mind and take it back. So she continued to have the same money problems as before.

Jane wrote the book quickly, and by July, when she and Grub had returned to Africa, she completed all but the final chapters. Not long after, she submitted the full manuscript to the publisher. And finally, in 1971, *In the Shadow of Man* went on sale in both England and the United States.

Shadow made a bigger impression on the general public than any of Jane's previous work. Even though National Geographic had published *My Friends The Wild Chimpanzees* four years earlier, they only marketed that book to Society members. *Shadow* was available to the general public, and it held widespread appeal. It was a feminist story of a woman taking on the challenge of living in the wild with untamed beasts, and learning from them. It was also an adventure tale, full of exciting accounts of a modern-day—and female—Tarzan.

The year 1972 held many changes for the Gombe Stream Research Centre, and Jane hardly had a chance to relax. Undergraduate students from Stanford arrived to begin their own primate research. Soon they were followed by undergraduates from the University of Dar es Salaam, in addition to the graduate researchers Anne Pusey, Mitzi Hankey, and Richard Wrangham. The camp had grown to also include six African field assistants, five of whom were considered chimp specialists and the sixth a baboon specialist. These men didn't write English and had little formal education—no scientific training at all—but they had proven their worth and were recognized for their abilities. Jane wrote, "My life settled into a regular pattern. The glorious solitude of the first couple of years was gone forever, and I often thought back on that time with regret. Yet it was a purely selfish regret—I could never have gathered, on my own, even a tenth of the exciting information that we were learning from the efforts of the students and the field staff."

Just as Jane's staff at Gombe was growing, Grub was growing—growing up. At five years old, his days were filled with swims, walks, and nature observations. He played with the children of the African staff members or from the nearby village. There were drawbacks, though, to raising a child in the forest. As much as Grub loved nature, he did not share his mother's ease with animals. He had nightmares about being attacked by a baboon and had several scary encounters with Gombe's poisonous snakes. Once, when Jane encouraged Grub to hand some toy plastic bananas to Flint, the ape took the toys and began walking away. A moment later, Flint returned and bit Grub's hand. Grub never really wanted to go near the chimps again after that episode.

Because they lived at the research center, Grub could not go to a regular school. Jane enrolled him in a correspondence program, which provided lesson plans by mail that she would teach to Grub. Though she sat with him every day to get him to do his schoolwork, it was a battle. She wrote to her family in Bournemouth in March 1972, "He gets through school fast . . . unless he is in a MOOD! Then we sit for 2 hours, him saying he won't do it, me saying Oh then we just have to stay here, what a pity. Then he does it for a few minutes just before I strangle him!"

All in all, Jane was becoming increasingly successful. She wrote scientific papers and gave lectures, and *In* the Shadow of Man was a best seller in the United States and England, and was translated into forty-seven foreign languages. Jane was even elected to the American Academy of Arts and Sciences, a society of distinguished scientists and artists from around the globe. She didn't know what to make of this, writing, "<u>I have yet to find out exactly how significant it is</u>, but I feel fearfully honored!"

Hugo, on the other hand, was as ambitious as Jane but less successful. His book *Innocent Killers* was literally stuck in the shadow of Jane's *In the Shadow of Man*. Jane noticed that Hugo was depressed, and in many ways, the National Geographic Society was contributing to that depression. Citing its rights to photos and film taken at Gombe while it was providing funding, the Society refused to grant Hugo permission to make his own film about Jane and Gombe. They also refused permission for a new film about Flo and her family. They even went so far as to deny Hugo's request to take photographs at Gombe for his personal use.

Hugo and Jane's personal life was suffering, and the two began to realize that, apart from an interest in animals, they did not have much in common. Jane enjoyed classical music and poetry; Hugo had little use for either. Jane was spiritual and Hugo was not, but when Grub asked a question about God, Hugo laughed without even considering Jane's feelings about the matter. Jane was deeply offended by his reaction. Furthermore, Jane felt that Hugo was not interested in her career as a scientist, did not take pleasure in her accomplishments, and felt a need to control their lives. Jane and Hugo separated, and retreated to different parts of East Africa—Hugo to the Serengeti and Jane to Gombe with Grub. Jane became Grub's full-time caregiver, an interesting parallel to her chimp research. After all, she had observed that adult male chimpanzees can be very doting toward young chimps, but the strongest bond in the chimpanzee world is between mother and child.

Jane did not have much time to focus on her marital problems, though, because that summer Flo had been fading. Jane estimated that Flo was close to fifty years old, and she was obviously ill. Jane wrote to her family, "She is, quite literally, a skeleton with some hairy flesh around it. She spends most of the time lying on the ground." During the third week of August, Jane found Flo's lifeless body, with Flo's son Flint staring listlessly at it. Flint was clearly brokenhearted, and Jane mourned as well; she wrote, "Although I had known the end was close, this did nothing to mitigate the grief that filled me as I stood looking down at Flo's remains. I had known her for eleven years, and I had loved her." For the first night, Jane watched over Flo's body, wanting to spare Flint the sight of his mother being torn and eaten by bush pigs. Each night for the next few nights, she carried Flo to camp and stretched the body on a pallet—right next to where a visitor, Irven DeVore, was attempting to sleep. In the mornings, the body was returned so that Jane could continue to record Flint's reaction and the responses of Flo's other children. Flint's grief was overwhelming, and he hardly ate or moved. By September 15, Flint was dead as well.

Jane wrote an obituary for Flo, praising the old matriarch and declaring that Flo had contributed a great deal to science. She wrote that she had "learnt much wisdom during my years of association with Flo. I owe her a personal debt of gratitude and, for me, Gombe can never again be the same." It was the first obituary for a nonhuman ever printed in the London *Sunday Times*, an honor to both Jane and to Flo. Unfortunately for Jane, the same morning that Flo's obituary appeared, she received news that Louis Leakey had passed away as well.

Louis was sixty-nine, and had not been well for some time. He was overweight, had already had one serious heart attack, suffered from arthritis, and hobbled around with a cane because of an unsuccessful hip-replacement surgery. Still, he was vibrant and had a number of projects, books, and lecture tours under way. In fact, he had been writing a book with Vanne—they were working on the finishing touches in London when Louis began complaining of tiredness. He went to the hospital, where an electrocardiogram seemed normal, but the next morning, Louis suffered another massive heart attack. He passed away at around nine o'clock the morning of October 1.

Louis had been a mentor, friend, and cheerleader for Jane for her entire professional life. He and Jane had remained in constant contact through letters, radio, and telegrams throughout her Gombe study. His passing was a great personal tragedy for her and much of her family. Jane remarked about her old friend, "Twentieth-century science would have glowed less brightly without Louis Leakey and his dynamic contributions. With his persistent determination, which yielded such a wealth of fossil material, with his vision of the wide scope of evolution, and with his ability to inspire others to continue his work and his ideals, he will, without doubt, take his place in history as one of the scientific giants of his century."

Jane tousles seven-year-old Grub's hair, 1974.

Eight

THE LOSSES OF 1972 seem to have inspired Jane to make major changes in her life. The first was to hire a new general administrator for Gombe in place of Hugo. Jane hired Emilie van Zinnicq Bergmann. She had met Emilie in 1971 in a village near Utrecht in the Netherlands, where she had worked as a veterinary technician. Other new people at Gombe arrived as well, including Stanford students David Riss, Jim Moore, Chuck de Sieyes, and Craig Packer. Life in the intimate quarters of the camp meant people got to know one another very well, and the friendships forged at Gombe lasted a lifetime. But sometimes the relationships went beyond friendship. David and Emilie met and fell in love at Gombe and eventually married. Jane had fallen for Hugo in those same forests, and even though Hugo was no longer in the picture, Gombe would work the same romantic magic for Jane again.

In February 1973, thirty-eight-year-old Jane became reacquainted with Derek Bryceson. Derek had stopped at Gombe years before when he was Tanzania's minister of agriculture, and now he had been appointed the director of national parks in Tanzania. Derek was tall and white-haired, an Englishman by birth but an African by choice. He had been badly injured in a plane crash during World War II, which left him with partially paralyzed legs. He had been told that he would never walk again. But he defied the odds and, with a walking stick, he managed to get around. He moved to Kenya after the war to become a farmer but soon became involved in politics. He had been one of the first white settlers in Africa to support Julius Nyerere, future president of Tanganyika (and later of Tanzania, when in 1964, Tanganyika and Zanzibar united to form a new nation). When Nyerere was elected president, he made Derek the only white member of his first cabinet.

When they met again, Jane was on another hunt for funds to support the research at Gombe.

The money from the previous year was running low, and new funding from the Grant Foundation was not due until November. She went to see Derek to discuss Gombe, and found him to be likable and far more sympathetic to her concerns than the previous parks directors had been.

A few months later, in May, Derek visited Gombe. Jane wanted him to see as much of the chimps as possible but worried about how Derek would make it to the camp's provisioning area with his difficulty in walking. She arranged to have him carried up, but Derek walked the whole way, and was rewarded with the sight of more chimps than the researchers had seen at that spot in months.

Derek helped Jane forge better relationships with government officials in Tanzania, including President Nyerere. Soon, Derek was making frequent trips to Gombe, and Jane was traveling to Dar es Salaam as well. She went on Gombe business, but inevitably saw Derek, too. As they got to know each other, Jane learned that Derek shared her love for music and literature and her spirituality. In fact, Derek encouraged her to read Bible stories to six-year-old Grub and to talk to him about religion, which she did.

Jane's staff noticed the closeness between the two, even though Jane was still legally married to Hugo, and Derek was married as well. But it was obvious that they were powerfully drawn to each other. On August 7, Derek and Jane met in Kigoma to run some errands before heading back to camp together. The errands took longer than anticipated, and they did not leave for Gombe until after dark. The pair decided to share some ginger wine to revive themselves—and ended up sharing kisses as well.

When Derek returned to Dar es Salaam, Jane and Grub followed him there for a holiday. Grub enjoyed playing on a beach without any chimpanzees or baboons to worry about, while Jane enjoyed every moment with Derek. They spent some more time together in September before Jane and Grub had to leave for Stanford.

The two occasionally spoke on the telephone and regularly exchanged letters. In December, they managed to meet up in person when Derek traveled to Stanford after a weeklong lectureship he had com-

pleted at Rhode Island University. The letters between
Jane and Derek discussed their love for each other, as
well as concerns they had about pursuing a relationship. Derek pressed Jane to move forward with him.
He wanted to leave his wife and Jane to leave her
husband.

Derek also wanted Jane to end her association with
Stanford so that she would not be separated from him
during her trips to America. Jane thought that Derek
did not understand how important her research was
to her and tried to explain her need to work—and the
importance of Stanford. Derek, though, continued to
pledge to do whatever was necessary to keep Jane with
him in Africa.

At the time, Jane did not realize how much Derek
was like Hugo. She thought that because Derek was
a powerful and influential man in his own right he
would not be jealous of or intimidated by her fame
and success, despite the clues that Derek was no more
comfortable with Jane's celebrity than Hugo had been.
It was too early in the relationship, however, for Jane
to see clearly beyond the haze of a newfound love.

ಬಂಧಬಂಧ

In early 1974, after returning from Stanford, Jane and seven-year-old Grub planned to go on safari to Ruaha National Park with Derek. They were flying there in a small Cessna plane when smoke began to come out of the instrument panel. They managed to fly another forty-five minutes, into view of the landing strip of the park. But suddenly, a herd of zebras wandered onto the strip, blocking them from landing. The pilot was too afraid to circle the defective plane and began to panic. He chose to go in for a crash landing on the far side of the Great Ruaha River, even though the plane was flying twice the normal landing speed. Derek, who had been a pilot himself, cried: "You're not going to try to land here, are you? Don't!" But the pilot ignored him, and the plane crashed.

As soon as the plane was on the ground, the pilot jumped out, leaving the engine running. Jane was terrified that the wrecked plane was going to burst into flames. Though everyone on board had survived, Derek's ribs were cracked. As calmly as she could, Jane managed to unbuckle Grub and ordered him to climb out of the wreckage. Derek was stuck in his seat—he was wedged in by luggage, his door was jammed, and his partially paralyzed legs limited his ability to get himself out. Jane began to frantically hurl the luggage away to free Derek. All the while, Derek joked with her, asking whether she was searching for a missing purse. Even through their fear, Derek charmed Jane.

The near-death experience helped Jane make up her mind about her marriage to Hugo. She realized that life was uncertain and that people should make the most of the time they have. She decided to divorce Hugo. After Derek divorced his wife, Bobbie, they would marry.

Jane and Derek worried that news of their crash, and the fact that they were vacationing together, would get out, so they knew they would have to speak to their spouses and children immediately. Derek's grown children had no idea about Jane, and while Grub knew that Derek was a good friend of his mother's, he did not understand the reality of Derek and Jane's relationship and how that would change his own family.

Hugo returned to Gombe at the beginning of February, independently wanting to discuss his and Jane's relationship. Hugo asked if Jane would leave Gombe for him, and, of course, Jane was not willing. Finally, they calmly decided that the marriage no longer worked. Jane would always say that her time with Hugo was worthwhile. In a 1975 interview with *Ladies' Home Journal*, Jane said that after their divorce she and Hugo "still work together [and] we're even better friends. We don't feel any bitterness. We had a jolly good time and we produced Grub. We achieved together more than we could have done separately."

At the end of March, Jane left for her spring term at Stanford. She and Hugo had decided that the divorce could be taken care of easily the next time they were both in Holland, and Jane wrote to Derek that the situation had "turned out well—amazingly and unbelievably well."

During her time in California, though, Jane began to worry that her relationship with Derek would not last. Most of their affair had been conducted through love letters and occasional telephone calls. Jane wrote to Derek, "I sometimes dread that you expect too much and that you will be disappointed and begin to regret the suffering that we are now causing. Yet it's too late to turn back."

Also, Derek was becoming more insistent about

Jane breaking her ties with Stanford and the United States. To Derek, Jane's American commitments were a waste of her time, and they kept the two of them away from each other. But much of the Gombe research was being done by Americans and supported by American money. Her heart was with Derek, yet Jane knew she needed Stanford.

At the beginning of May, Jane left Stanford as scheduled. She spent a few days with her family in Bournemouth and then met Hugo in Holland to process their divorce. Jane wrote to a friend, "Hugo & I went through with our plans—it took 5 mins in a courtroom in the Hague. We are great friends. Still."

Afterward, Jane headed back to Gombe and found the atmosphere of camp to be quite jolly. In her absence, several new people had arrived, including three new Stanford students, Curt Busse, Grant Heidrich, and Kit Morris; a postdoctoral scholar, Larry Goldman, and his wife, Helen; and a new Gombe staff member, Etha Lothay. David Riss had also come back to write up his previous research for publication.

In June, Jane and Grub traveled to the Ngorongoro Crater for a holiday with Hugo, a trip Jane enjoyed a great deal. She wrote home on June 21, "It is such a relief to be just friends with him—I can't tell you. He keeps doing the things that used to make me feel so trapped & desperate—& I feel so happy that it doesn't matter any more. We are getting on famously."

Jane did not, however, spend much time with Derek that summer. After Ngorongoro, she went to a conference and then managed only eleven days with Derek in August, in Dar es Salaam and Ruaha National Park. Then she returned to Gombe in time for a visit by the American actress Candice Bergen. Bergen had been asked by *Ladie's Home Journal* to write a piece on Jane, and Jane had agreed. The article would make her work even more familiar to the general American public.

Some time during the first week of February 1975, Jane and Derek had a quiet civil wedding ceremony with only Grub present. In their life together in Tanzania, Jane was, for the most part, the less famous of the two. Derek was a popular politician, a member of the Tanzanian parliament and, for a long time, the only democratically elected white politician in all of Africa. Derek was recognized by Tanzanian citizens, and Jane was usually known not as a ground-

Jane with the actress Candice Bergen at Gombe, 1974.

breaking scientist, but as Mrs. Bryceson, Derek's wife.

For a time after the wedding, Jane's life was fairly routine. Since she and Derek did not take a honeymoon, Jane and Grub returned to Gombe on February 9. Derek followed soon after, in time for Grub's eighth birthday on March 4. The couple continued to live apart as necessary, with Jane in Gombe and Derek in Dar es Salaam.

On Monday, May 19, a catastrophe occurred at the park. Around eleven thirty at night, while Jane was sleeping, a boat carrying forty armed men came to shore near the park headquarters at Nyasanga, a half mile south of the research station. The intruders were dressed in military fatigues and carried rope, grenades, and AK-47s. They captured two of the three park rangers who lived at the park headquarters; the third ranger escaped and was able to warn the two American researchers, Ann Pierce and Jim Baugh, who lived at the park headquarters to be closer to the animals they studied. He urged them to flee, but Pierce and Baugh headed toward the research station to try to warn the people there about the intruders.

The armed men reached the research station first and captured American students Emilie Bergmann, Stephen Smith, Carrie Hunter, and Barbara Smuts, and Gombe staff member Etha Lothay. Jane and Grub were still in their cabin some distance away. The kidnappers interrogated their prisoners and the nearby villagers, trying to find any other white people, but every person they questioned bravely told the same lie: that there were only those four white people who were already captured. Soon, the kidnappers loaded the Americans into a boat and sped down the river with them, leaving the rangers and Etha behind.

In the tumult that followed, Jane was woken and told of the kidnapping. She immediately wrote a note to request help from the police and dispatched park rangers to deliver it. She could only tell them that the attack happened—at that point, no one even knew the identity of the kidnappers. Unfortunately, there was nothing more to do until dawn, when the police and people from the parks department would be awake and able to receive radio messages.

By seven o'clock the next morning, Jane had reached the parks department by radio; thirty minutes later, she spoke to Derek, who was in Dar es Salaam. Derek immediately met with Tanzania's minister for home affairs, who made sure that other government officials were informed about the incident. Derek flew out to Kigoma to meet Jane. In the meantime, the rest of the white students and researchers, along with Jane and Grub, were evacuated from Gombe to Kigoma by the Tanzanian police. They were only allowed back in under heavy police escort to gather their belongings.

Derek and Jane did everything they could to locate the hostages. They flew a small parks department plane around the countryside, hoping to glimpse some kind of encampment that might be hiding the kidnappers, but were unsuccessful.

Stanford's president sent word that all the remaining American students should leave for Nairobi for their own safety. The university was, in effect, prohibiting them from doing any more research in East Africa. But Jane's students wanted to show their support for their kidnapped friends and chose to wait with Jane and Derek at their home in Dar es Salaam. Finally, on May 24, American ambassador William Beverly Carter received a message that Barbara Smuts had been released unharmed and was in Kigoma. She was flying to Dar es Salaam the next day.

A small crowd of people, including Jane and Derek, met Barbara at the airport before she was whisked off to the American embassy. By that time, the kidnappers had been identified as members of the Parti de la Révolution Populaire (PRP). The PRP was a rebel group trying to overthrow the government of Zaire to establish their own state under their leader, Laurent Kabila. Barbara carried letters from the PRP demanding money and weapons, and the release of certain political prisoners. If their demands were not met, the kidnappers were prepared to kill Emilie, Stephen, and Carrie. Fortunately, though, Barbara reported that the hostages had been treated well while she was there. The kidnappers frequently shook their hands and fed them three meals a day.

The pressure was building, even among the people trying to secure the release of the remaining students. The American embassy issued a statement saying that it was Tanzania's job to deal with the PRP and that the American ambassador could not and would not negotiate with the kidnappers. The Tanzanian government responded by proclaiming that it had no responsibility in the affair and would not negotiate with the PRP either.

Stanford professor David Hamburg arrived from the United States along with the parents of Carrie Hunter and Stephen Smith. It became clear that Jane, Derek, and the other private citizens involved would have to negotiate directly with the PRP, and Hamburg insisted that he and the fathers of the two kidnapping victims be involved. Derek, however, was intent on keeping Jane isolated from the other people involved. He felt that Jane had no role in Tanzanian politics apart from being his wife, and he did not let Jane contact Hamburg or anyone else involved in the situation independently. Jane, anxious to support her husband, accepted Derek's judgment. She also had a tendency to hope for the best, and Hamburg, who admitted that he was depending on her to be a leader through the crisis, came to believe that she did not really accept how serious the situation was.

On June 20, a full month later, Derek and Hamburg began to negotiate with two men who represented the PRP. Derek took the lead, and talked for three hours. He assured the PRP representatives that Tanzania would release any PRP members held in its jails if the kidnappers released the hostages. By the end, he felt confident that a good relationship between the two sides had been formed, and he believed that he could resolve the situation without having to pay any ransom. But he was wrong.

Hamburg had invited the fathers of Carrie and Stephen to the negotiation, disregarding Derek's objections that involving the fathers would automatically bring up the subject of ransom. Unfortunately, Derek was right. All of his reasoning fell to the wayside, and the kidnappers demanded $460,000.

The total amount was collected based on Carrie's father's credit. The small-denomination British pounds were stacked in a strongbox, and on June 27 the money changed hands. But the PRP reneged on the deal and only released Hunter and Emilie. On July 5, Jane wrote home to say, "We do feel that Steve [Smith] will be okay, though. Just that it is going to take time—hopefully nothing else—to get him back. Isn't it lousy, though, for him to be left on his own. . . . Sitting around, waiting, trying to do things but managing to get very little done, has become a way of life." It took another week for Smith's release, after two prisoners were released from Tanzanian jails, and then the nightmare was over.

Nine

AFTER THE KIDNAPPING, there were a lot of changes at Gombe. For one, no American students or staff remained there—they did not return after being evacuated during the hostage crisis. All the field research was now conducted by the Tanzanian staff. The research itself was mainly limited to one project studying baboon swimming and the task of maintaining the long-term records of the chimps in the banana-provisioning area. Certain individual chimps were also still followed.

At the beginning of Jane's chimpanzee study, she had believed that the chimps were somehow nicer than human beings, that they exhibited the positive aspects of humanity, such as building communities and cherishing the bond between parent and child, but did not take part in the negative aspects, such as warfare. But now Jane documented some behavior that changed her mind.

In August and September 1975, Jane's Tanzanian field staff observed one of the chimps, Passion, and her children, Pom and Prof, kill and eat other chimpanzees. In one especially disturbing incident, Passion seized and ate another mother's infant chimp. Jane wrote, "We know that five [infants] . . . (including Gilka's two) were killed and eaten by Passion and Pom, and we suspected . . . three [more] were also." Jane thought the behavior was gruesome, and she and the other researchers noticed that even the other chimps found the cannibalism abnormal. Most of them avoided Passion and her children.

Another type of violent behavior was witnessed as well. What was essentially a war began between two neighboring communities of chimpanzees, the Kasekela group, which lived on the northern side of the reserve, and the Kahama group, which lived on the southern side. Initially, both groups formed one large community, but the Kahama group broke away to form a smaller community and treated their former

The chimp called Mike sitting at the top of Kasekela Falls.

community members as trespassers. The males in both groups were aggressive when they met members of the other community. If a patrolling group came across a weaker chimp or group, the encounter was often lethal. These killings continued until late 1977, when the Kasekela group completely annihilated the Kahama apes. Jane realized that chimpanzees were more like humans than even she, who had studied them for so long, had realized. Like a human, each chimp had a dark side.

In the May 1979 issue of *National Geographic*, Jane published an account of the violence she had ob-

served. About her article, Jane wrote, "When I published the first observations of intercommunity killing
at Gombe I came in for a good deal of criticism from
certain scientists. Some critics said that the observations were merely 'anecdotal' and should therefore be
disregarded. This was patently absurd. . . . Even among
scientists who accepted the Gombe data, there were
those who believed that it had been a mistake to publish the facts; they thought that I should play down the
aggressiveness whenever possible. . . . It was my first
experience with the politics of science, the pressure
to publish or not to publish for political, religious, or
social reasons." Jane was not, nor had she ever been,
interested in political opinions. She wanted to learn
about the Gombe chimpanzees and all the facets of
their behavior. So, just as she had ignored the critics
who said she shouldn't name the chimps she studied,
she ignored these scientists who thought that some
observations shouldn't be shared.

While Jane's understanding of chimpanzee nature
evolved, there were other changes in her life as well.
In 1975, Grub was eight years old, and Jane realized

that he needed to go to a real school with more discipline and order than she could provide in Africa. Jane and Derek proposed the idea of going to school in England and spending holidays in Africa to Grub, and he agreed. He left for England that fall. Jane wrote, "He lived with Vanne at the Birches. I have always been horrified at the English custom of sending small children, from overseas, off to boarding schools 'back home.' But this was different. The Birches, with Danny, Vanne, Olly, and Audrey, was an extension of Grub's home." Despite the rationalization, Grub's absence was difficult for Jane. She found the house quiet and lonely without him. She could hardly bear to go into the room attached to her office that she and Grub had used as a schoolroom, writing to him that "I don't like going into because I always feel so sad you are not here. Though I <u>am</u> glad someone else is teaching you spelling & writing and not me."

Until Grub finished school, the schedule was roughly the same: he spent school terms in England, Jane traveled to Bournemouth to be with him at Christmas, and Grub spent summers in Africa, splitting his time between Gombe with Jane and the Serengeti with Hugo. During Grub's visits at Gombe, Jane would sometimes feel overwhelmed by the demands of motherhood, but as soon as he left, she felt a sense of loss at not being a mother.

Jane had a lot to balance, between her professional life, motherhood, and marriage. Early in their courtship, Derek had wanted to sever Jane's relationships with the Americans with whom she worked. During the hostage crisis, many of the Americans involved found Derek to be hostile. Some even believed that he was trying to use the situation to get the Americans out of Gombe. When Jane went to Stanford in October 1975, she felt a great deal of hostility from her peers. She heard the rumors that Derek would rather have let the kidnapped students die than pay any ransom and that she had somehow slipped into the jungle and abandoned her students when the kidnappers entered the camp. People whom Jane had considered friends were now giving her the cold shoulder. In fact, one of her colleagues even canceled the house rental she had arranged before she arrived in California, forcing Jane to spend her first night there on the flea-ridden carpet of a last-minute sublet. When her teaching responsibilities were completed at the end of the fall term, Jane left her Stanford position.

During this trying time, Jane's spirits were raised when two old friends, Prince Ranier di San Faustino of Italy and his wife, Genevieve, came to visit her at Stanford. Their warm companionship was a welcome change from her suspicious colleagues. They also came up with an idea to solve Jane's financial problems. Prince Ranier proposed that Jane create the Jane Goodall Institute for Research, Conservation, and Education, a charitable foundation, to provide a steady income for the research and upkeep at Gombe. Jane agreed, and they discussed who would be approached to be trustees and board members. Work began immediately to make the Jane Goodall Institute a reality.

The foundation was established in the United States because Jane's experience had shown her that the bulk of the available funding came from the U.S. By 1976, the foundation was up and running. While the bank accounts did not start with much money, funds were trickling in, which was a first step toward Gombe's financial independence.

In late 1976, Jane learned that the Grant Foundation was no longer going to provide the annual $25,000 that she needed to run Gombe. It was planning to cut its grant to $10,000, forcing Jane to raise the remainder through donations, grants, and the money she earned from giving public lectures. In fact, Jane's public speaking engagements became an important source of fund-raising for the Jane Goodall Institute. Jane was sometimes criticized for this mode of fund-raising by other conservationist groups. They grumbled that Jane used her celebrity status to gain the lion's share of the available grants and donations. Despite this, Jane began regular speaking and fund-raising tours throughout the United States.

The more Jane traveled, the more hostilities emerged in her marriage. Jane felt Derek's protectiveness, which she had once found so comforting, had turned into possessiveness. Derek did not like Jane to go out with friends or to have any type of social life apart from him. In fact, by late 1979, the marriage was so troubled that Jane privately concluded that it would not last much longer. Everything that she had hated about being with Hugo seemed to be repeating with Derek. But sadly, there was no time to deal with their problems, because in early 1980, Derek began suffering from abdominal pains and had trouble digesting.

X-rays in Dar es Salaam showed a dark mass that needed to be removed, so Derek went to England for surgery, with Jane by his side. The surgeon informed Jane that Derek had cancer. He had three months to live.

Suddenly, the marital problems that Jane had so recently worried about were inconsequential. All she could think about was how she would face life without Derek. For days she told no one but her sister-in-law Pam Bryceson and Vanne about the diagnosis.

When Jane finally told her family about Derek, once again Vanne was her strength. Vanne came to London and encouraged a desperate Jane to find some alternate treatment for Derek's cancer. Jane called friends in Dar es Salaam and asked them to look for an African witch doctor who might have a treatment. She dispatched an Indian acquaintance to find a root she had heard about that might help. She also learned about a doctor in Germany who treated cancer patients with a controversial drug called laetrile. By July, Derek was in Hanover, West Germany, being treated with laetrile by Dr. Hans Nieper.

At first, Jane was convinced that Derek was getting

better, writing to friends that he was no longer in pain and that they had crossed a hurdle. The hope that the laetrile gave them provided Jane and Derek an opportunity to reconnect. They talked for hours, listened to music together, and prayed together.

The British surgeon, however, had been correct in his diagnosis. Derek grew progressively worse, and he began to need morphine to bear the pain. Jane pleaded with his doctor not to keep him alive when he was in so much pain. On October 11, Jane was by Derek's side when he passed away. She listened for her husband's last breath and then climbed into the bed by his side to hold his body close one last time.

In November 1980, Jane brought Derek's ashes back to Dar es Salaam. She later wrote, "It was a harrowing time, especially when, at Heathrow, I was handed the casket that contained his ashes. All that was left of his mortal flesh in one small box. Even now, nearly twenty years after his death, I can vividly recall the utter horror I experienced when I took it into my hands." A memorial was held for Derek, and afterward Jane intended to take his ashes by boat to one of their favorite spots, an island in the Indian Ocean where they had often snorkeled.

But when Jane and her guests boarded the boat to go to the island, everything began to go wrong. It was raining, making it impossible to see anything. The boat did not have enough gas and so did not reach the island. It took a great deal of time to unscrew the top of the box holding Derek's ashes. Jane thought she would sink the box and a wreath by weighing them down with a stone, but no one had rope to tie the box and stone together, and no one had a knife to cut the rope that did not exist. Jane said of the occasion, "I'm sure Derek was laughing."

At Christmas, Jane returned to England to spend the season with Grub, now thirteen years old, and the rest of her family. That winter, Vanne underwent successful surgery to replace a heart valve. The new heart valve had been harvested from a pig, and in honor of the pig that had given its life for Vanne—and because her mother was now, at least, part pig—Jane began to put together a book of pig facts and pictures to give to Vanne. When Jane returned to Africa at the end of January, the pig book was a welcome hobby for her evenings after she worked on chimp and Gombe business.

By May, Jane was back to a routine at Dar es Salaam, and at the end of the month, she headed to Gombe for a few weeks. It was a difficult place to be since Jane had met Derek there, but over time it became less painful as Jane refocused on the chimps. She wrote to her family in May, "Well, I really did have a lovely time at Gombe. . . . I spent a lot of time wandering in my old haunts, the Peak, and along my old tracks . . . Quite delicious, and I felt about 25 again! I found I was very fit, despite no mountains for so long!" That summer marked the first time that Jane, at age forty-seven, returned to her mind-set of 1960, feeling free to follow her curiosity.

But Jane was not completely free at Gombe. The financial difficulties continued, and Jane was actively looking for new donors to the Jane Goodall Institute to support the Gombe research. Eventually, in May 1983, Gordon Getty, who had been president of the Jane Goodall Institute since 1979, proposed a challenge—if Jane raised $250,000, he would match the amount to create a half-million-dollar endowment for the institute. An endowment is a permanent fund created to finance an organization or institution, and with an endowment in place, the Jane Goodall Institute would have a permanent source of income. Jane was able to meet the challenge with money from her lectures and contributions from donors. She looked forward to ending the "hand to mouth way of living" that she had grown used to for so long.

Jane also found the time to turn her attention to another project. Back in 1968, she had published a scholarly book summarizing her research called *The Behaviour of Free-living Chimpanzees in the Gombe Stream Reserve*. A decade later, she began working on an updated edition, but by 1982, the project had taken on a life of its own. Instead of being a simple update of a slim, single-volume book, it turned into a two-volume encyclopedia of sorts, summarizing all of her work with the chimps since she started at Gombe. Published in 1986, it was called *The Chimpanzees of Gombe: Patterns of Behavior*, and was more than 650 pages long.

Jane dedicated the book to those who had been most influential in starting her career. Her dedication read: *For my mother Vanne, for the chimpanzees of Gombe themselves, and in memory of Louis Leakey.* While the book summarized everything she had learned after decades of studying chimps, in truth, Jane's work was not finished. In many ways, her real work was just beginning.

Ten

WITH THE JANE Goodall Institute's endowment in place, Jane was able to think about new projects. In 1984, she came up with the idea for ChimpanZoo. Jane was very concerned that captive chimpanzees in zoos all over the world were kept in prisonlike cages, with steel bars and concrete floors, and with nothing to play with or entertain them. Her research had shown that in the wild, chimps lead emotionally rich lives and need the same kinds of nurturing that humans do to be happy. She wanted to improve zoo conditions for captive chimpanzees. She planned to create a program that would provide zoos with nesting materials, artificial termite mounds, bedding, and other things that the apes might see in the wild. That way, university professors and students could study the

Jane at the 2006 Day of Peace in Los Angeles, California.

captive chimps and compare their behavior to what was seen in the wild.

Though the Jane Goodall Institute bore her name, the decisions about what projects to fund were not made solely by Jane but by the institute's board. She felt strongly about ChimpanZoo, but the board did not agree at the time that it was a good investment. By now, Jane had an income separate from her fundraising efforts—from royalties from her books, prizes that she was awarded, and speaking fees. As a result, she decided to fund the first year of ChimpanZoo herself, using her own money. It turned out to be a success, and the Jane Goodall Institute eventually began officially funding ChimpanZoo. In 2007, the program was under way at twenty locations all over the world and the research is ongoing. Notably, the program continues to do what Jane originally intended—make conditions better for zoo chimpanzees.

Jane's next big project also had to do with protecting chimps. In November 1986, fifty-two-year-old Jane attended a conference sponsored by the Chicago Academy of Sciences called "Understanding Chimpanzees." She went to the conference as a scientist—

arguably the most important chimpanzee researcher there—but she left as an activist, committed to conservation and education.

At the conference, Jane and many other scientists agreed to form an organization to lobby governments around the world on behalf of chimpanzees. It was named the Committee for Conservation and Care of Chimpanzees, or CCCC, and Jane agreed to be its celebrity public representative.

One of the first things Jane did while working with the CCCC was increase protection for chimps in the wild. People knew that baby chimpanzees needed for research were exported from West Africa. They also knew that the adult chimps related to the babies were often killed in the process. Experts estimated that for every baby collected, ten other chimps were killed. In 1988, Jane persuaded Senator John Melcher of Montana to add an amendment to a bill, prohibiting the use of funds from the National Institutes of Health for any project involving chimpanzees caught in the wild. This provision forced researchers to stop supporting the trade in wild chimpanzees. With fewer buyers, the people who had been harvesting the baby chimps had less reason to continue to do so at the expense of other chimpanzee lives.

In 1990, Jane spoke to Secretary of State James Baker about how research demands were contributing to wild chimp deaths because of the way baby chimps were harvested. Secretary Baker assured her that as long as he was in office, the U.S. Department of State would uphold the American policies protecting wild chimps that Jane had worked with Senator Melcher to bring about.

In addition to political activities, Jane began touring research facilities throughout the United States that worked with chimps. Her goal was to identify which labs employed practices that were detrimental to their research animals. She felt that speaking out against such practices would help end them.

One of the first labs that Jane toured was at SEMA, Inc. in Rockville, Maryland. Jane had watched a videotape called *Breaking Barriers*, secretly recorded inside the SEMA labs, which showed brutal conditions for the research chimps. Baby chimps were removed from their mothers at birth, raised for eighteen months in a nursery, and then placed into small cages in pairs. These cages were two feet high and less than two feet wide or deep, so small that the chimps could barely turn around. By age two, the chimps were moved into single boxes called isolettes (forty inches high, thirty-one inches deep, and twenty-six inches wide). The isolettes were supposed to separate the animals from each other to prevent the spread of airborne viruses. In reality, they condemned the animals inside to a life deprived of most sights, smells, tastes, sounds, and touches.

The video shocked Jane, and she openly criticized SEMA and their practices. In response, SEMA invited Jane to tour its labs in March 1987 in the hope that she would change her mind about its research operation. However, the tour just confirmed the conditions on the tape. Jane tried to explain that chimpanzees needed social relationships, activity, and opportunities for play. Her words fell on deaf ears.

Jane's next stop was the Laboratory for Experimental Medicine and Surgery in Primates (LEMSIP) in Tuxedo, New York, in May 1988. She discovered that the infant chimps at LEMSIP had toys, a jungle gym, windows, and emotional comfort from human caretakers. But as soon as the chimps grew old enough, they were taken from the coziness of the nursery to individual cages five feet wide and five feet deep. Unlike the chimps at SEMA, the ones at LEMSIP could see one another through the aluminum bars, but for the most part, they had no physical contact with other chimps.

Jane was saddened by the cages she saw at LEMSIP. After meeting one of the LEMSIP chimps, Spike, Jane broke down and began to cry while kneeling in front of the ape. He reached through the bars of his cage to feel the tears on Jane's cheek. Jane's guide, LEMSIP's chief veterinarian, Jim Mahoney, saw this and broke down as well. When Mahoney walked away, clearly upset, Spike reacted badly—perhaps he thought that the strange woman who had come to visit had somehow hurt his friend. Spike grabbed Jane's hand and bit her right thumb. The tip of the thumb had to be amputated.

Instead of discouraging Jane, this incident only reinforced her desire to make the lives of lab chimps such as Spike happier and more fulfilling. Her efforts, however, were sometimes met with criticism. In a 1990 interview, she described the hostility she felt from some sections of the scientific world: "Behind it [the hostility] is a feeling, 'If Jane gets her way and we are forced to make these improvements in the living conditions of the chimpanzees, it's going to cost a lot of money. And that's the thin end of the wedge—having made the improvements for chimps, she's going to want to make improvements for monkeys, and dogs, and cats.' And you bet I am!" Through the Jane Goodall Institute, Jane eventually established an enrichment program at LEMSIP to teach lab technicians about the capabilities of chimpanzees. Within a few years of Jane's first visit, the research chimps were given items such as unbreakable mirrors, willow twigs, and toothbrushes to explore and play with. Jane still felt it was awful that the animals lived in cages, but she admitted that the chimps were happier with the stimulation and soon looked forward to human visits, in anticipation of rewards and new toys.

Jane didn't forget about wild chimpanzees with her new focus on laboratory conditions. In 1992, she was instrumental in the creation of reserves for wild chimpanzees. Years before, the American oil company Conoco had wanted to prove that it was committed to protecting the environment while harvesting coal. To this end, the company pledged to build, with Jane's help, a chimp sanctuary in the People's Republic of Congo to help orphaned chimps. In December 1992, the Tchimpounga sanctuary opened and twenty-five chimps, including young orphans, ex-pets, and former zoo animals, moved into their new home.

Involvement in Tchimpounga brought Jane familiar headaches. Once again, money was a problem. Conoco covered the cost of the construction— $660,000—and the Jane Goodall Institute took responsibility for the $100,000 annual costs. In 1993, however, the Jane Goodall Institute essentially ran out of funds and could not support Tchimpounga or any other projects. The institute's investments were not doing well, and the United States economy was weak. This meant fewer people were contributing to charities. But because Jane believed in the project, she again used her own funds to keep it running. In 1990, Jane received the Kyoto Prize in Basic Science, the Japanese equivalent of a Nobel Prize, which came with a cash award of $50,000. Jane transferred this $50,000 to cover the operational costs for the sanctuary, and then once again began fund-raising to keep Tchimpounga running.

Jane's work with chimp sanctuaries and bettering conditions in labs stemmed from her interest in improving the world for animals. But she also recognized that many people need as much help as animals do. In 1989, Jane was touring a secondary school in Dar es Salaam, talking to young people about chimp communication, tool making, and other behaviors. She announced that any students who had additional questions should leave their names—and she got a long list. She invited fourteen of the curious students to her house a few weeks after the lectures to talk about animals and conservation. By the end of the visit, the students had decided to form a club for young people dedicated to conservation, protecting animals, and improving the world for humans and animals. The club was called Roots & Shoots.

As Jane explained, roots, which are often unseen

under the ground, provide a strong foundation for even the largest trees; and shoots, which at first appear frail, will always grow toward light, regardless of any barriers in the way. This was a powerful metaphor for what Jane wanted to nurture in the first Roots & Shoots club. As she has said to many audiences, "You make a difference. Your life matters and it's up to you to save the world and each one of us has this mission." Today, there are more than seven thousand Roots & Shoots clubs in schools and communities in eighty-seven countries around the world. Jane, who remains as involved as she can, wrote, "Young people, when informed and empowered, when they realize that what they do truly makes a difference, can indeed change the world. . . . Because I believe that nothing is more important, I am devoting much of my time to developing [this] program for youth."

Conservation was an important part of Roots & Shoots, but Jane also realized that the best way to stop habitat destruction was to create a program that helped people in rural villages, near the habitats of wild animals, survive without taking land away from their animal neighbors. In 1994, Jane and the Jane Goodall Institute established the Lake Tanganyika Catchment Reforestation and Education project, or TACARE. The goal was to reach out to the people who lived in the villages near Gombe and help them improve their lives while conserving their natural environment. TACARE offers savings and credit programs, plants new trees, and helps develop crops to bring in income. In addition, services such as family planning, water sanitation, and HIV/AIDS education are provided. There are also Roots & Shoots programs for children supported by TACARE.

Within a decade, more than thirty villages near Gombe were participating in the TACARE program. More than a million new trees were planted, and more than 150 students had received funding to attend secondary school and college. TACARE is a success and is now being used as a model for other projects in the Congo and Cameroon.

Every project Jane has undertaken in her life, from her initial study of the Gombe chimps to Roots & Shoots and TACARE, has grown to be something much larger than she had originally envisioned. Both the CCCC and the Jane Goodall Institute have become powerful protectors of animal rights, and Roots & Shoots and TACARE continue to expand. Jane still has the same work ethic that she always has. The young woman who once trekked the mountain trails of Gombe from dawn until nightfall now, more than four decades later, travels more than three hundred days a year.

Fame followed Jane from the earliest steps of her career, but that has always been less important to her than the work itself. She consistently tries to keep her personal life out of the spotlight, though her celebrity makes that difficult. Jane appears more and more in popular culture. She has appeared on cable channel specials, voiced a character on the television series *The Wild Thornberrys* and been parodied on *The Simpsons*, and was the subject of a cartoon drawn by noted cartoonist Gary Larson. She is stopped for autographs and is considered a hero.

Jane is very close to her son, Grub, who lives in Tanzania with his wife and three children. He is still not very interested in his mother's work with the chimps, but his son, Jane's grandson, is passionate about animals. In 2000, Hugo, who had gone to live with Grub in Tanzania, passed away. It was a sad time for Jane, but not as devastating as Vanne's death in 2001. In speeches, Jane still honors Vanne, saying in late 2003, "The person, though, that I want to pay the most tribute to is my mother. She died three years ago, but I still feel her very much around, and throughout my entire life she was my greatest inspiration and support. Of course, I miss her terribly."

On Jane's seventieth birthday in 2004, she attended a Roots & Shoots festival in Pasadena, California. More than fifty Roots & Shoots groups from the Los Angeles area came to meet Jane, share their projects, and listen to her speech. Jane wore a ruby turtleneck and quilted jacket, and looked vivacious and strong. Someone asked Jane what the secret of her youth was. She responded, "There's so much to do."

Today, Jane Goodall spends ten months of every year circling the globe, bringing a message of community, conservation, and hope to anyone who will listen. Long ago, she dreamed of traveling to Africa to see wild animals in their natural habitats. Now, she dreams of preserving those animals and our planet for generations to come.

In one of Jane's many speeches, she spoke about her dreams. She said, "The value of the individual, that every single day we wake up, we impact the world around us, we can help, and we get the choice as to what sort of impacts we want to make. . . . Let's take this message away from here . . . let's reach out to as many others as we can. . . . So that when our great grandchildren are born, and theirs, there will be blue sky and trees and birds singing, and some chimpanzees swinging, and some chimpanzees in Africa."

Jane photographed in 2001.

Source Notes

INTRODUCTION

"for over half . . .": van Lawick-Goodall, *In the Shadow of Man*, 16.

CHAPTER ONE

"whirly kind of . . .": Peterson, *Jane Goodall*, 7.

"I went berserk . . .": Peterson, *Jane Goodall*, 17.

"I must have . . .": Goodall, *Reason for Hope*, 6.

"If you look . . .": Goodall, Aspen Institute speech.

"it was my . . .": Goodall, "Dangers to the environment," 71.

"We have lovely . . .": Goodall, *Africa in My Blood*, 15.

"Find a fairly . . .": Goodall, *Africa in My Blood*, 18.

"She was bossy . . .": Peterson, *Jane Goodall*, 49.

"her whole philosophy . . .": *Enough Rope*.

"I want to . . .": Goodall, *Africa in My Blood*, 55.

"In those days . . .": Goodall, *Reason for Hope*, 31.

"I could go . . .": Goodall, *Reason for Hope*, 35.

CHAPTER TWO

"I <u>still</u> find . . .": Goodall, *Africa in My Blood*, 76–77.

"it was all . . .": Goodall, *Reason for Hope*, 42.

"apparently enchanted him . . .": Goodall, *Reason for Hope*, 44.

"Here was the . . .": Goodall, State of the World Forum speech.

"It was a . . .": van Lawick-Goodall, *In the Shadow of Man*, 18.

"It was wild . . .": Goodall, State of the World Forum speech.

"The great aim . . .": Goodall, *Africa in My Blood*, 108.

"he is so sweet . . .": Goodall, *Africa in My Blood*, 109.

"when I got . . .": Goodall, *Africa in My Blood*, 120–21.

"a token of his love": Goodall, *Africa in My Blood*, 119.

"My situation here . . .": Goodall, *Africa in My Blood*, 118.

"All my life . . .": Goodall, *My Life with the Chimpanzees*, 45.

"I've been waiting . . ." and "When he put it . . .": Goodall, *Reason for Hope*, 55.

"He hunted and . . .": Goodall, *Reason for Hope*, 54.

CHAPTER THREE

"First I have . . .": Peterson, *Jane Goodall*, 162.

"luckily for my . . .": van Lawick-Goodall, *In the Shadow of Man*, 21.

"At that time . . .": Goodall, *Reason for Hope*, 63.

"He explained, regretfully . . .": van Lawick-Goodall, *In the Shadow of Man*, 22.

"I have never . . .": van Lawick-Goodall, *In the Shadow of Man*, 23.

CHAPTER FOUR

"What had I . . .": van Lawick-Goodall, *In the Shadow of Man*, 26.

"How lucky I . . .": van Lawick-Goodall, *In the Shadow of Man*, 55.

"In between the . . .": van Lawick-Goodall, *In the Shadow of Man*, 32.

"His expression was . . .": Peterson, *Jane Goodall*, 194.

"absolutely no fear": Peterson, *Jane Goodall*, 198.

"in exactly human . . .": Peterson, *Jane Goodall*, 200.

"I found that . . .": van Lawick-Goodall, *In the Shadow of Man*, 39.

"People often ask . . .": Goodall, "My Life Among Wild Chimpan-
    zees," 281.

"George said he . . .": Goodall, *Africa in My Blood*, 164.

"on several occasions . . .": van Lawick-Goodall, *In the Shadow of
    Man*, 44–45.

"Now we must . . .": Peterson, *Jane Goodall*, 212.

"I was, by . . .": van Lawick-Goodall, *In the Shadow of Man*, 56.

"I now climb . . .": Goodall, *Africa in My Blood*, 167.

"Mostly the actors . . .": Goodall, *Africa in My Blood*, 172.

"What a birthday . . .": Goodall, *Africa in My Blood*, 175–76.

"some experience of . . .": Peterson, *Jane Goodall*, 252.

"getting in the . . .": Peterson, *Jane Goodall*, 254.

"I just can't . . .": Peterson, *Jane Goodall*, 259.

CHAPTER FIVE

"The word was . . .": Peterson, *Jane Goodall*, 263.

"When I began . . .": Goodall, "Learning from the Chimpanzees,"
    2,184.

"ignored the admonitions . . .": Peterson, Jane Goodall, 277.

"My future is . . .": Morell, "Jane Goodall," 50

"The work she . . .": Peterson, *Jane Goodall*, 296.

"The significance of . . .": Peterson, *Jane Goodall*, 297.

"this woman has . . .": Peterson, *Jane Goodall*, 286.

"He IS a . . .": Goodall, *Africa in My Blood*, 221.

"We are a . . .": Peterson, *Jane Goodall*, 308.

"quite ghastly": Peterson, *Jane Goodall*, 316.

"our conversation is . . .": Peterson, *Jane Goodall*, 327.

"very happy with . . .": Peterson, *Jane Goodall*, 332–33.

"I had found . . .": van Lawick-Goodall, *In the Shadow of Man*, 77.

"found a palm . . .": Goodall, *Africa in My Blood*, 267.

"WILL YOU MARRY . . .": van Lawick-Goodall, *In the Shadow of Man*, 90.

"dreaded most terribly . . .": Goodall, *Reason for Hope*, 84.

CHAPTER SIX

"simply the most . . .": Goodall, *Africa in My Blood*, 280.

"I rushed about . . .": van Lawick-Goodall, *In the Shadow of Man*, 92–93.

"have a most . . .": Goodall, *Africa in My Blood*, 302.

"own special little tent": Goodall, *Africa in My Blood*, 294.

"because chimpanzees are . . .": Goodall, *My Life with the Chimpanzees*, 91.

"How sad that . . .": Peterson, *Jane Goodall*, 371.

"the most qualified . . .": Goodall, *Africa in My Blood*, 334.

"we were horrified . . .": van Lawick-Goodall, *In the Shadow of Man*, 133.

"should really fox . . .": Goodall, *Africa in My Blood*, 369.

"so exciting we . . .": Goodall, *Beyond Innocence*, 8.

"It was unutterably . . .": Goodall, *Beyond Innocence*, 17.

"The whole affair . . .": Goodall, *Beyond Innocence*, 28.

"Bells and trees . . .": Peterson, *Jane Goodall*, 409.

CHAPTER SEVEN

"Hugo & I . . .": Peterson, *Jane Goodall*, 419.

"most extraordinary life": Peterson, *Jane Goodall*, 426.

"I had to choose . . .": Goodall, *Reason for Hope*, 88.

"There is no . . .": Goodall, *Reason for Hope*, 90.

"I still cannot . . .": Peterson, *Jane Goodall*, 434.

"If only [Davis] had . . .": Goodall, *Reason for Hope*, 92.

"Hugo and I . . .": van Lawick-Goodall, *In the Shadow of Man*, 239.

"Figan is still . . .": Goodall, *Beyond Innocence*, 171.

"My life settled . . .": Goodall, *Reason for Hope*, 86.

"He gets through . . .": Peterson, *Jane Goodall*, 490.

"I have yet . . .": Peterson, *Jane Goodall*, 491.

"She is, quite . . .": Goodall, *Beyond Innocence*, 167.

"Although I had . . .": Goodall, *Through a Window*, 31.

"learnt much wisdom . . .": "Old Flo, the Matriarch of Gombe, Is Dead."

"Twentieth-century science . . .": "Louis Leakey's Legacy."

CHAPTER EIGHT

"You're not going . . .": Goodall, *Reason for Hope*, 99.

"still work together . . .": Bergen, "With Jane Goodall in Africa," 70.

"turned out well . . .": Peterson, *Jane Goodall*, 530.

"I sometimes dread . . .": Peterson, *Jane Goodall*, 533.

"Hugo & I . . .": Peterson, *Jane Goodall*, 536.

"It is such . . .": Peterson, *Jane Goodall*, 537.

"We do feel . . .": Peterson, *Jane Goodall*, 559.

CHAPTER NINE

"We know that . . .": Goodall, *Reason for Hope*, 115.

"When I published . . .": Goodall, *Reason for Hope*, 118–19.

"He lived with . . .": Goodall, *Reason for Hope*, 90.

"I don't like . . .": Peterson, *Jane Goodall*, 570.

"It was a . . .": Goodall, *Reason for Hope*, 161.

"I'm sure Derek . . .": Peterson, *Jane Goodall*, 581.

"Well, I really . . .": Peterson, *Jane Goodall*, 586.

"hand to mouth . . .": Peterson, *Jane Goodall*, 590.

CHAPTER TEN

"Behind it is . . .": "Reaching Across the Species Barrier" interview.

"You make a . . .": *CNN Newsnight*.

"Young people, when . . .": Goodall, *Reason for Hope*, 242.

"The person, though . . .": Goodall, "Dangers to the environment," 71.

"There's so much . . .": Peterson, *Jane Goodall*, 679.

"The value of . . .": Goodall, State of the World Forum speech.

Bibliography

Bergen, Candice. "With Jane Goodall in Africa." *Ladies' Home Journal* 92 (February 1975): 32–36, 70.

CNN Newsnight Aaron Brown, February 11, 2005. http://transcripts.cnn.com/TRANSCRIPTS/0502/11/asb.01.html

Chu, Jeff. "The Queen of Gombe." *TIME Europe* 164 (October 11, 2004): 60.

Enough Rope with Andrew Denton, Episode 113. http://www.abc.net.au/tv/enoughrope/transcripts/s1691815.htm

Fuller, Alexandra. "Jane Goodall." *Vogue*, August 2005, 204.

Goodall, Jane. *Africa in My Blood*. Edited by Dale Peterson. New York: Houghton Mifflin Company, 2000.

———. *Beyond Innocence* New York: Houghton Mifflin Co., 2001.

———. "Dangers to the Environment: Jane Goodall's Speech to the Commonwealth Club of California." *Vital Speeches of the Day* 70 (November 15, 2003): 71–79.

———. "Environment: Reasons for Hope." Speech, Aspen Ideas Festival, The Aspen Institute, Aspen, Colorado, July 6, 2005. http://www.aspeninstitute.org/site/c.huLWJeMRKpH/b.1106779/k.45AA/Dr_Jane_Goodall_at_Ideas_Fest.htm

———. "Learning from the Chimpanzees: A Message Humans Can Understand." *Science* 282 (December 18, 1998): 2184–2185.

———. "Life and Death at Gombe." *National Geographic*, May 1979, 592–621.

———. "My Life Among Wild Chimpanzees," *National Geographic*, August 1963, 272–308.

———. *My Life with the Chimpanzees*. New York: Simon & Schuster, 1996.

———. "New Discoveries Among Africa's Chimpanzees." *National Geographic*, December 1965, 802–31.

———. "Old Flo: The Matriarch of Gombe Is Dead." *The Sunday Times*, London, October 1, 1972, 9.

———. "Protecting the Web of Life." Presentation, State of the World Forum, New York, N.Y., September 9, 2000. http://www.simulconference.com/clients/sowf/plsimcasts/plenary15.html

———. "Reaching Across the Species Barrier." Press conference interview reproduced in *Orion*, Spring 1990. http://arts.envirolink.org/interviews_and_conversations/JaneGoodall.html

———. *Through a Window*. New York: Houghton Mifflin Co., 1990.

Goodall, Jane, with Phillip Berman. *Reason for Hope*. New York: Warner Books, 2000.

Haugen, Brenda. *Jane Goodall*. Minneapolis, Minn.: Compass Point Books, 2006.

Jane Goodall: My Life with the Chimpanzees. Narrator, Jack Lemmon. Producer, Judith Dwan Hallet. Writers, Patrick Prentice, Lynn McDevitt. Washington, D.C.: National Geographic TV, 1990.

"Louis Leakey's Legacy: Celebrating the Centennial of His Extraordinary Life and Finds," AnthroQuest Online, Fall 2003. http://www.leakeyfoundation.org/newsandevents/n3.jsp

Miss Goodall and the Wild Chimpanzees. Narrator, Orson Welles. Executive Producer, Robert C. Doyle. Producer and Writer, Marshall Flaum. Washington, D.C.: National Geographic TV, 1965.

Morell, Virginia. "The Discover Interview: Jane Goodall: The Woman Who Changed the Way We Think about Animals Reflects on What She's Learned from Her Adoptive Chimpanzee Family." *Discover* 28 (March 2007): 50.

Peterson, Dale. *Jane Goodall: The Woman Who Redefined Man*. New York: Houghton Mifflin Company, 2006.

Rauber, Paul. "People Say That Violence and War Are Inevitable. I Say Rubbish (An Interview with Jane Goodall)." *Sierra* 91 (May–June 2006): 42–44.

Selim, Jocelyn. "Why Chimps Still Deserve Our Respect:

'We're Not the Only Creatures with Personalities, Minds, and Feelings.'" *Discover* 25 (May 2004): 18–20.

van Lawick-Goodall, Jane. *In the Shadow of Man*. London: William Collins & Sons Co Ltd, 1971.

Vanderpool, Tim. "Going Ape: The Chimpanzoo Program Enables More Scientists to Join the Goodall Fight." *Tucson Weekly*, October 12, 2000.

Index

Note: Page numbers in *italics* refer to photographs.

Photo Credits

Page 14: Reprinted by permission of National Geographic

Page 18: Library of Congress, Prints & Photographs Division,

LC-DIG-ppmsca-03434

Page 36: Library of Congress, Prints & Photographs Division, NYWT&S

Collection, LC-USZ62-109642

Page 55: Photograph by Fotos International © Hulton Archive/Getty Images

Page 65: Library of Congress, Prints & Photographs Division, NYWT&S

Collection, LC-USZ62-122227

Page 96: Reprinted by permission of National Geographic

Page 109: © Hulton Archive/Getty Images

Page 137: Photo by Curt Busse

Page 152: © Hulton Archive/Getty Images

Page 163: Photo by Curt Busse

Page 172: Photo by Curt Busse

Page 184: © Frank Armstrong

Page 199: © Maria Cecilia Camozzi 2007